How to
Broker Bu &
E

Step by step guide to Starting a Home based Trucking Freight brokerage business

From LLC filing to Getting your First Client

Fred R. Dorsey

GALICIA
PUBLISHING HOUSE

Published by: Galicia Publishing House

Support@BarberryBooks.com

Design & Cover by Olivia O'Neal

First Edition

TABLE OF CONTENTS

Dedication

This book is for my wife, who listens to me ramble endlessly about work when I know she doesn't truly care. She has never complained, though. Thank you, Laura, for all that you've done to help me reach my success level

The level of success *we* have.

Special shoutout to Markus, who got me into the business. I wouldn't even know what a freight broker *was* all those years ago if you hadn't taken me under your wing, and I appreciate everything you did for me. I'll never forget it and never stop trying to repay your kindness.

INTRODUCTION

Take a moment and look around you. Think about the coffee table in your living room, the chair or couch you are sitting on, and even the car you drive. Most of these common, everyday items didn't start in your house. They were made in a factory, facility, or workshop. They then got put on some form of transportation, be it a boat, train, truck, or plane, and were moved to another location. Sometimes, this involves multiple methods of transportation.

When you think about it, that new piece of furniture or clothing may have traveled more than you have within the same time frame!

With a more connected society, and online shopping taking over so much retail space, shipping will become more central to daily life. There is almost no getting around it.

This means that freight brokers, and the freight industry as a whole, are more needed than ever before. Projections have this industry continuing to grow and expand in the coming years, so there is more than enough room for all of us to carve out a piece of the pie and enjoy success.

If you want to *stop* working for other people and *start* taking control of your life and success by starting a freight broker business, this book is for you.

So... Who Can Become a Freight Broker? What Does it Take, Really?

I get this question from well-meaning folks who don't grasp what a freight broker actually does. If you're thinking the same thing, don't fret. By the end of this book, I promise you will be an expert on the topic.

The truth is almost *anyone* can be a freight broker. It only takes a few important personality or situational details to succeed in the business.

One: You have to *want* to be a freight broker. If you're reading this, I assume you have that checked off.

Two: You want to work for yourself. You don't want a boss breathing down your neck, and you're ready for independence.

Three: You want to work from home for the most part. I know some people hate the 'work-from-home lifestyle, but you have to be able to get up out of bed, move to your home office, and start work. That's important. If you're *not* self-motivated to create a better life for yourself, this might not be the position for you. Sounds harsh, but very true.

Four: You're willing to learn, adapt and change as the market changes. This isn't necessarily a business where you will use the same basic strategy for the rest of your career. As technology advances and shifts, you will also need to shift with it. If learning new things and trying different strategies doesn't appeal to you, this may not be the career move for you.

If most or all of these things sound like you, great! You've passed the test, and yes, you could probably become a freight broker. Of course, it's not quite that easy... but it's not necessarily hard, either.

Freight Transportation

"What exactly *is* freight?"

I get this question a surprising amount from well-meaning folks who don't think about it before they ask it. Freight is basically cargo, so anything that needs to travel any distance. As I mentioned above, look around you: nearly everything in your home office, your kitchen, your bathroom, your bedroom, all of that needed to travel from Point A to Point B. Sometimes, it went from Point A to B, to D, to F before making its way to you.

Freight transportation is moving those things where they need to be. The industry is also known as *shipping*, the term most people are familiar with. Within the industry, though, shipping generally means *by ship*, as the name suggests. Obviously, in the past few hundred years, we have diversified how we move things around. However, plenty of cargo still gets tossed onto a ship to travel across the ocean.

There are three main types of fright transportation that you will become familiar with as we read through this book.

By ship or *shipping*, you are loading cargo and goods onto a ship and transporting them across the world. You may think this is an outdated method of transportation. Still, a huge number of goods (staggeringly high) get transported via ship each day. If you don't believe me, look at what happened in the Suez Canal in 2021. One of the busiest trade routes in the world got blocked by a stuck ship, and nearly $10 billion in cargo was held up while it was fixed. All boats.

About 90% of the world's trade gets transported via ship, with over 100,000 commercial ships hauling and moving. That's a lot of ships and a lot of goods.

If a country has its own ships to transport goods, it is called a merchant navy or sometimes a merchant marine. It doesn't have to be countries specifically importing or exporting goods. Large-scale businesses often run or charter out large cargo ships to transport their goods.

The ground method of transportation is probably what folks think of, especially in the US, when they think of freight transportation. Ground or land, shipping is done either by train or truck. Most of this cargo comes *from* a plane and moves *to* ground transportation to reach its final destination.

Ground transportation becoming common was a huge reason countries with limited coastlines could even get appropriate supplies. Think about it: if you only have a few miles of coast, but you have a lot of lands, you need good ground transportation to feed, clothe, and provide goods to your citizens.

Air transportation is exactly how it sounds: you load it onto a plane and fly it where it needs to go. It's not nearly as popular as using a ship or ground method, but it has gained popularity over the years. Unsurprisingly, air transportation is faster than ground or even ship.

Because of the fuel price and the high skillset needed, plus the upfront cost of a cargo plane, this tends to be the most expensive method. If you need something fast and don't care how much it costs, air transport is the way. Otherwise, the cost is often prohibitive for most companies or people.

You also will run into the word *intermodal* in this business. This essentially uses multiple means of transportation to move goods, like taking them from a ship and putting them on a train. Generally, when this term is used, an intermodal shipping container is used. That means when transporting the goods, the container itself is plucked straight from the first method and dropped into the second, with no need to move around containers or packaging. The goods get delivered right to the door of the recipient.

What a Freight Broker Really Does

Shippers, or people that have cargo, need carriers, or people that move cargo to move their stuff. Without a proper carrier, the cargo isn't going anywhere. Cargo, in this case, could be any number of things - furniture, electronics, steel beams. There is really no shortage of cargo.

A freight broker works sort of as the middleman in this situation. The shipper often needs a liaison between them and the carrier to coordinate pickup and drop-off and ensure everything goes smoothly.

"Can't they do that themselves? Why does my position even exist?

Great question... sort of. Some large companies Think big companies, like Ikea, Coke, and Pepsi.

But thousands and thousands of smaller companies don't have a full-time need for that position, so it's cheaper and easier to outsource it to someone like you. You won't fund your new business working with just one shipper or one carrier, but instead, working with many shippers with all sorts of crazy cargo to move.

More and more businesses are popping up each day, needing someone like you to help them out.

"Is there more to it?"

Sure! You're not just going to facilitate the connection between shipper and carrier. Still, you will also be handling insurance issues, transport paperwork (just so much paperwork!), and logistic issues. It's not the shipper's problem to deal with oddly shaped cargo. It's *your* issue to solve and find a carrier.

You're also helping carriers. Many smaller carriers don't have the time, money, or resources to source shippers, plus they deal with paperwork. Being able to pick up the phone when it rings and send a truck out ASAP to that cargo is great, and it can also help carriers fill gaps between other contract jobs.

Wait, Who Are You?

Yet another good question! Sorry, I didn't introduce myself earlier: I'm Frank MacNeil, a freight broker.

I've owned my own business handling freight for over 15 years now, and in that time, I've seen a lot of other freight brokers come and go. I've made my fair share of mistakes (some I'll even share as words of warning about!), and I've learned a lot.

I started the business about 20 years ago when a family friend named Markus Lowe introduced me to all things freight. He knew I was struggling and unhappy in my current job, and he had a freight broker business. I think he took pity on my wife, who he watched grow up, and wanted to help us both build a better, more fulfilling life together.

I worked with Markus for several years, learning all about being a freight broker and how to make connections with people before setting out on my own with his blessing. There was more than enough market for the both of us, after all.

Markus is happily retired now, and his son runs the business. I can't thank him enough, and in part, I'm writing this book because of him. I wouldn't be here without him, not just literally, but because he helped me. It only feels right that I can do the same for someone else in the position I was in. Unhappy with my job, unhappy with the trajectory of my life, and looking for something more.

If you identify with this statement and want something more, then know I am writing this book for you. I'm here to help you the best I can with all the knowledge I've gained to get you started in this job and find something more.

How to Use This Book

I have written this book for you to be a guideline for starting your freight broker business, top to bottom. My experience in this industry has taught me what to do and what not to do. I'm here to help you skip some of the minor and major mistakes I have made or seen others make when building their business.

From writing a business plan to legally registering your business, gaining – and keeping! – clients, and so much more. This should be your comprehensive guide.

The book is broken down into two parts. The first part is **the overview** or the wide view of the job. What exactly goes into being a freight broker, why you might be a good freight broker and the skills you need to succeed. Don't worry if you don't know everything right away! I'll teach you or show you where to find the knowledge you need to succeed.

The second part is the **detailed work**. This is the bulk of the book and contains the nitty-gritty of setting up and running your business daily. This covers taxes, bookkeeping, marketing, reaching out to potential clients, and disaster handling.

It's not always going to be easy, but so few things are worth doing. With this book and a lot of personal drive and ambition, you *can* grow a successful business. There are few limits to how big you can get, only how much desire you have.

The only truly limiting thing in this business is *you*?

Ready to begin?

Chapter 1: Everything You Should Know about Being a Freight Broker

This is your one-stop shop for all things freight brokers. We're going to start with common terms, like shippers and carriers, dive deep into how freight brokers make their money, and touch on some important skills you need to succeed as a freight broker.

Keep an open mind as you read this section, even if you feel like you can skip immediately past it. It's important to have a solid foundation to move forward confidently. You *don't* want to miss something major in this chapter and cost yourself a lot of time and money later.

What is a Shipper?

This term is used extensively in this book and your daily business life. A shipper is a business, or an individual, that owns the cargo they need to move. They are also sometimes referred to as consignors.

The Types of Carriers

The carrier is a company or an individual transporting the goods from point A to point B. This can be someone driving, flying, or shipping your goods, depending on where the cargo needs to go.

There are two main types of carriers you are going to run into. The common carriers and the contract carriers.

A common carrier is a company or an individual transport provider licensed. It offers its services to whoever wants to pay. They are not bound by any contract that states they can only work for a single person and are free to take as many 'jobs,' or shippers, as they can handle. Think of a common carrier as a freelance agency.

A contract carrier, on the other hand, transports via a relationship or contract. This is usually a much longer-term relationship, predetermined by a contract. That means a contract carrier signed a contract with Business X to work for a set amount of time under certain circumstances.

The third type of carrier you probably won't see a lot in your daily routine is something called a global freight forwarder. These folks handle shipment across countries, sometimes crossing land borders, sometimes going over water, etc. It all depends on where the cargo needs to go.

Global freight carriers essentially play by different rules than your standard carriers. Some are restricted to their specific countries or just a few countries.

IDEAL CARRIERS TO WORK WITH

As I previously mentioned, you want a good safety rating when looking for carriers. But a little *pro tip* from someone who has done this a while is to form good, lasting relationships with carriers that can handle a variety of transportation, including flatbeds, traditional trailers, and more.

You never know what your shipper will need or where they will need it. You don't want to be caught potentially losing a big shipper or opportunity because you have restricted yourself to narrow availability carriers.

It would help if you also considered the licensing your state requires carriers to have. Each state will be different, so I would encourage you to double-check what your state and the surrounding states have before you start connecting with carriers. Once you *know* what they need, legally, you can ensure they have those things.

I'll talk more about this later, but it's good to keep it in mind as you start. Again, your reputation is on the line here. It's beyond important you keep up with it.

Great question! As a glorified middleman, it might seem like a freight broker isn't seeing much financial action. After all, the carrier is getting the biggest portion of this. They *are* technically doing all the hard work. Is it even worth it?

Of course, it is; anyone who has been in the business long enough knows logistics makes a ton of money. It's an industry that is one of the wealthiest but quieter, subtle wealth, not in-your-face flash, glitz, and glam.

YOU'RE THE SALESMAN MIDDLEMAN

You are no different from the average middleman in any other business. Think of yourself as being in sales, but you're selling yourself, the ease of your service, and your quality to shippers. If you can market *yourself* and how you can help businesses grow, you will grow.

Like in sales, you will have a flat amount of money each week or month you are guaranteed to bring in. Instead, the amount of cargo you haul and your gross margin is going to be what you are taking in. In some months, this number can be very high. Others it may be very low.

Let's talk for a minute about that: **gross margin**. The gross margin is what you make from a single job after all other expenses *for that job* are complete. This isn't your bottom line, as you still need to pay utilities to keep the lights on and your internet running.

Essentially, your gross revenue for each shipment handled is this:

Price charged to the shipper – price paid to the carrier = gross margin

Easy, right? A carrier will charge you $3,000 to transfer the shipper's goods. You are going to charge the shipper $4,000 to do it. Your equation would look like this:

$4,000 charged to the shipper - $3,000 paid to the carrier = $1,000 gross margin

In this industry, though, this is never really a flat income. What you make each month will change because what the carriers will charge you for cargo movement constantly changes. The shipping industry is incredibly volatile, and many factors can be at play regarding its costs.

In that way, you are also *sort of* a financial broker, too. You're finding the best deals for you and your shipper, buying and selling assets.

Ultimately, the biggest thing you can keep in mind while doing this job is that your sales to shippers don't *really* matter. Whether you're getting $50,000 a month from shippers or $250,000, your gross margin is what you will see. That is the number that ultimately matters.

SIGNS OF A GOOD FREIGHT BROKER

There are a few things that you can do to set yourself apart, especially when you are just starting your business. As I mentioned, this business has a lot of room for growth. However, you must ensure you follow all the rules and make smart decisions. Run in guns blazing without any concept of what a good, quality freight broker brings. You're going to be out of business before you know it.

There will always be another freight broker your clients can turn to if you drop the ball. Never forget that.

A GOOD FREIGHT BROKER IS PROFESSIONAL

Get used to this word because I will repeat it approximately 2 dozen times in the following chapters. A good freight broker is always professional, easy to talk to, and reach. Networking and word of mouth will be huge for growing your business without investing much money in marketing. There's no faster way to *stop* growing than to be unprofessional.

It's really easy to forget this the longer you're in business. Perhaps you get cocky, and someone speaks to you the wrong way on the phone. Maybe you have a bad day and end up lashing out at someone asking you the same question for the third time. Maybe you're just *too comfortable* in your position in your home office and forget who you're talking to.

Could you not do it, ever?

Professionalism is your number one priority when you step into your office or answer your phone. People will respect that, the value that, and continue to choose you over other options *because* of it.

A GOOD FREIGHT BROKER GROWS RELATIONSHIPS

The clients and relationships you create and build within your business are not disposable. Very rarely are you doing *just one* ship for someone and never talking with them again. It would help if you approached every single interaction you have as building a long, lasting partnership with a company.

This kind of mentality you're working with to grow will benefit you at every step.

A GOOD FREIGHT BROKER IS FLEXIBLE

Finally, a good freight broker is *flexible*. If you want to be stuck in your ways and run your business the same way day in and day out, you will have a bad time. This really isn't the business for you.

Technology changes and you need to change with it. You may have to adapt to what you're doing or how you're doing it to keep up with the market.

Seasonality is also important to keep in mind. Many of us have a 'busy season' and a 'slow season. It's not a *dead* season, but when a winter storm rolls in for the third time in a month, there's probably not a lot of shipping and traveling you can even do with cargo. Remember to be *flexible* during this time, and you'll end up just fine.

THINGS A GOOD FREIGHT BROKER ALWAYS DOES

This is not an optional list, in my opinion. It would help if you stuck with the following rules to be successful, gain clients, and keep everything running smoothly.

THINK LOGICALLY ABOUT CARRIERS

This might seem obvious to seasoned professionals in this business. Still, it's super important- something newcomers don't always consider. It would help if you were very thoughtful with how you select your carriers.

Approximately 50% of your job is simply logistics at a certain point. If your shipment size is unusual, you need to think outside the box to accommodate that – this isn't a situation you "might" run into. It's something you'll absolutely need to handle regularly.

If you can set yourself up as someone who isn't afraid of a challenge like this, you will surely get repeat clients.

INSURED, ALWAYS

Your cargo should always be insured, all of the time. Talk with everyone involved during every step of the process to ensure that the cargo being transported is insured properly based on the estimated value (your shipper should be disclosing this to you) and that the carrier has appropriate liability coverage in case something happens.

I cannot stress enough that it only takes one bad situation to bankrupt your business, even a successful one.

NEVER TRUST TOO GOOD TO BE TRUE

You'll run into a situation sooner or later when contacting a carrier. They'll offer you an absurd rate far lower than you expected. It is tempting to jump on that and line your pockets with the extra money. However, be wary.

In my experience, carriers that can offer very low rates have a tradeoff: a poor safety rating.

You can argue that things happen on the road and no one is 100%, which would be true. However, if a carrier has a safety rating outside a reasonable error margin, there is a big problem. This could be with how they keep up with their trucks, treat their employees, or entirely.

No matter: if you choose a cheaper carrier with a poor track record or safety rating, you will be paying for it. Once you assign cargo to a carrier, your reputation is on the line as much as theirs is. Blaming the carrier for an issue you arguably should have seen coming will never fly, so be very careful with the carriers you choose and the prices you accept.

A Sidenote on This: In the last 3-5 years, an alarming trend has popped up in our circle; crime rings posing as carriers. Does it sound like a bad made-for-TV movie? Yes. Is it really happening? Also, yes. This is essentially a stolen identity situation.

A decently run criminal organization will set itself up as a carrier. Their safety ratings will be checked out, which might seem above board. However, they use fake motor carrier numbers to get in the door. Then they end up stealing the actual goods. Always double-check and vet your carriers before using; don't just trust what someone says.

Some Essential Skills

While I truly believe many people can make it in this industry and see success, it is important to know what you are getting into. Certain skills and even personality traits can help you be more successful and generally do better. Many of these don't have to be inherent, but you must work on them to find your place.

COMMUNICATION IS A MUST

Are you a person that dreads picking up the phone to answer a call? Do you hate calling a company to discuss something? Does opening your email make your stomach hurt?

I'm not here to judge, but I am here to warn you that this might not be the business for you. I spend a lot of time on the phone and in my email discussing logistics, scheduling, and more. I also have to build a rapport with these folks because you often work with the same people over and over again. Even when I'm not in the mood to be social, have had a rough morning, or am tired, I've got to pick up the phone and get it together.

If you don't think you can handle communication in nearly every part of the job, this might not be the best choice for your long term. Again, not a judgment – simply a fact of the job itself.

PEOPLE SKILLS MATTER, TOO

This goes hand in hand with communication: how you talk to people matters in this business. I have seen incredibly smart and driven people fail hard simply because they couldn't seem to handle being polite, normal human beings that could connect with others.

The relationships you build in this business last you a long time, and daily interactions are important. You can cultivate these skills even if you are not a traditional people person. I did.

I never considered myself great with people, but starting this business helped me understand what it means to connect with vendors and clients in a meaningful way. I started writing down important notes and questions to ask to help build deeper relationships (for instance, if someone I communicated with regularly told me their wife was sick, I would make a note to ask how they were the next time we talked).

Another aspect is simply being respectful. This isn't the most refined industry in the world, and you might confuse that with being able to speak your mind all the time. Just because we don't work on Wall Street and all wear expensive suits *doesn't* mean we can be rude or aggressive on the phone. In polite conversation, keep any polarizing opinions to yourself until you 'clock out and generally abide by basic business rules. This will see you the best success in building, and maintaining, good business relationships.

ORGANIZATIONAL SKILLS

You must be able to stay organized and neat. I will discuss this more in a later chapter, but it is a skill you need to start cultivating right now if you don't already have it.

As an owner, you are in charge of all work that goes through your business. You become everything your business needs, including a financial planner and a scheduler. If you don't keep organized, you easily get overwhelmed by everything you need to do and miss something important, like an order or request.

I will include strategies to help you succeed in a later chapter, but for now, know that it is very important to stay on top of every part of your business!

MANAGEMENT SKILLS

"But I don't have any employees, just me. Why should I even worry about management skills?"

Yes, it's true. You're probably running a one-person show. However, you *are* also a manager. And no, I'm not just talking about managing yourself. This isn't some pep talk from an online influencer. As a freight broker, you are managing every single shipping task given. This can easily get overwhelming, depending on how much you have going on at one time.

Having good management skills to delegate if needed, put off when you can, and prioritize are all essential to running a successful business. Some of this comes with time, and learning what a priority versus what isn't required you to be willing to learn is.

STRATEGY COMES INTO PLAY, TOO

Just as important as management is the ability to think strategically and act on those thoughts. There are a lot of 'links' in the supply chain, and knowing how to work them and what moves you may need to make to get something from A to B is important.

Unlike some of these other skills, this isn't an inherent skill you were born with. Some people are a little better at it than others, but it's something you work on every single day. Thinking creatively and critically will help.

LOGISTICAL THINKING

Is thinking *logistically* different from thinking *strategically*? Yes, and it's something else you need to either be good at or learn to be good at. People contact freight brokers *because* they need logistics. They cannot handle it themselves and need someone to think logistically and act as an in-between.

When handling logistics, you must think about the best routes for your client's needs and work with the information given to make the right decisions. This is yet another skill that will come with time.

MULTI-TASKING

Some of us were born multi-taskers, being able to juggle numerous projects or topics without a lot of stress. The rest of us need to learn that skill: and fast.

Multi-tasking successfully is vital to the continued growth of your business because you are doing pretty much all of it yourself. You need to wear multiple hats and do multiple jobs. You will be handling more than one client at a time, and you have to be able to mentally switch lanes at a moment's notice.

Practice this skill daily in every aspect of your life, and avoid things that don't help you multitask. That means I cannot watch television or listen to talk radio while I am actively handling work. My brain cannot process those words *along with* the task at hand. It simply takes too much of my bandwidth. For you, it could be setting reminders for other things at hand, making realistic goals, or even making sure you get up and walk around every hour. That sounds counter-intuitive, but it could give your brain the refresh it needs to get moving.

THE ABILITY TO LEARN

I struggled with how to phrase this skill. Still, the ability to learn new things and overcome challenges is absolutely essential to growing your business. You will not grow or succeed if you are unwilling to learn new skills and technology and implement new strategies.

This business isn't *just* about making phone calls and connections. You need to log into a new system, learn it when the need arises, and pick up a new skill without a lot of complaints, dragging your feet, or struggles.

If you're unwilling to adapt, you won't make it far. It's as simple as that.

Things You Don't Need to Know But Will Learn Here

There are a lot of 'other' skills that people may tell you you need to know. You don't *need* to know these immediately, but you need to learn them eventually.

Bookkeeping and accurate records are essential for your business's continued growth and success.

Negotiating with a client or carrier to ensure everyone is getting a fair cut will be very important in your business strategy.

Marketing is vital. Without a good marketing strategy and action plan, how will anyone know what you have to offer or that you even exist?

Compliance is important, and not following city, state, and federal regulations can sink a business faster than anything else. In some situations, you may argue that it's not your job to know all these rules, and you wouldn't be wrong – but knowing them will save you a lot of hassle in the long run.

If any of that sounds scary, don't worry and keep reading. I will tell you how to handle it all soon enough.

Chapter 2: Why Should You Consider Being a Freight Broker?

The job outlook for a freight broker is promising since it is the fastest-growing occupational category within the transportation industry; 29% compared to other occupations. As the economy improves and online shopping increases in popularity, freight brokers are becoming more in demand than ever. But outside of that, I can give you more reasons to become a freight broker.

Be Your Own Boss

If you become a freight broker, you choose to become your own boss and call all the shots. You can easily start as a single person and add employees as you grow. This gives you more time for the things you love, like spending time with family and friends, going on vacations, etc.

Low Start-Up Costs

If you have good credit, then you can often start a freight broker career on less than $5,000. The reason is that you can start from nothing and add on to your workspace and coverage as you want.

Low Overhead Expenses

If you're working alone from home, you'll save a lot of money on overhead costs. Most of your time is spent negotiating with shippers and carriers or researching and tracking shipments on the computer. A freight broker can keep their monthly expenses as low as $400-$500.

Unlimited Earning Potential

The freight industry is booming, and the only limit to your income is how committed you are to success. As e-commerce grows and flourishes, there is plenty of business for new freight brokers. There are plenty of opportunities for you to earn a lot of money. This means that it is a growing business.

The more you grow your freight brokerage business, the more you increase your position in the industry. This means you are constantly building new contacts. This leads to a job that has never-ending expansion potential.

A Family Business/Legacy

If you have a family, then a freight brokerage can be an excellent way to provide for the family and allow the whole family to get involved. You can start teaching your children about the job and pass it along to them as a family legacy.

Chapter 3: The Plan for Business Success

This is the first step to starting *any* business, not just a freight broker business. Getting a good foundation of a business plan to set yourself up for success is essential and will give you the best chance.

This is a step I see a lot of new business owners skip because they aren't looking to get funding from investors or share their business plans with others. Therefore, they feel they don't need to make one at all.

A business plan is a good idea for several reasons. It lays out your goals in your business clearly, helps you stay on track, and ensures you take your business seriously. By already dedicating the time to writing down your business plan, you are essentially just setting yourself up for success.

It will also help *others* take you seriously, which is a huge benefit.

The Basic Steps to Building a Business Plan

There are seven main steps in building a quality business plan. You need to take each step one at a time. I recommend grabbing a notebook, pulling up a document on your computer, and working on each step *as you* read this chapter. You can return and refine it later.

If you only want to skim this now, that is completely fine, but come back later with your notebook to get writing. You can also search for the business plan of a specific brand or company you admire. If they are publicly owned, you may be able to find it buried deep in the press section of their site!

Back to the plan, the seven main elements are:

-Goals
-Target Market
-Product
-Positioning
-Pricing
-Financial Projections
-Exit Strategy

Let's break this down piece by piece. It seems like a lot to work through, but each section doesn't have to be long or terribly detailed.

Your Goals

What are your goals for your business? *Why* are you starting this, and what do you hope to achieve? This is also where you're going to go on about *what* a freight broker actually is and what the job entails. This section can be as short or as long as you would like, but it should be comprehensive of your goals for the business and what you plan to do.

Setting good goals is very important to not just your business plan but your business. All successful businesses in every market have goals they set and want to achieve. These goals vary, of course, based on the business, but it's a defining factor.

Your goals are going to change the longer you are in business. You will hit some goals, create new goals, and realize that some goals aren't realistic. As you grow and change, new goals need to be made.

Goals serve several purposes. They keep you focused and oriented towards the future and give you something to work towards. It's easy to float by and not *push* in your business without goals, so setting good goals will help grow your business and make you even more successful.

The biggest mistake I see new businesses making when setting their goals is setting unrealistic expectations for your business. Look, it's nice to dream, but you're *not* going to blow up and make a million dollars your first year. Not unless something really, really incredible happens. You probably won't sit down and pull in ten jobs within ten minutes without any actual work.

Setting *realistic* and attainable goals is vital to your success. As you hit these goals, you can continue to set bigger and better goals, but breaking them down into realistic, attainable segments is important.

There is a set system that you are taught in business school to set good goals for your business. This is called SMART goals. I recommend you take some time when you set goals for your business and use the SMART system.

SMART is an acronym that stands for specific, measurable, achievable, relevant, and time-bound. Each is equally important, and if you're willing to stick with me for a bit, I can break each down.

You must follow this when setting goals, and you must *set goals* for your business. This is an important aspect of running a business. You are a business owner by becoming a freight broker and following these steps.

CREATING A SPECIFIC GOAL

When writing out goals for your business, you want to ask yourself: is this goal specific enough? "I want to be successful," "I want to be sought out in my field," and "I want to be the best" are all admirable goals, but they're not very successful. What does being successful mean to you? What does being sought out even mean?

Break down your goals. Where is your goal? What is it within that goal that you want to make happen, and how will you know when you hit it? What *resources* do you need to hit your goal? What limits are there within your goal?

Why does this goal matter to me? Why does it matter to the business? Who else is involved in the goal?

If you have a goal but cannot answer these questions and make it specific, then it is not a good enough goal for your business. Stop, rework it, and try again.

CREATING A MEASURABLE GOAL

If you cannot determine when you successfully hit your goal, have you actually *hit* your goal? Creating a measurable goal is an important part of goal setting because if you can't accurately measure it, you will keep moving the goalpost and never *actually* hit your goals. This is incredibly disheartening.

Ask yourself, how much will it take for me to get there? How will I know *when* I've reached my goal? What process do I have to go through to hit this goal, and how many items, tools, or things do I need to achieve it? What will it look like when I have, in fact, hit this goal?

Seems silly, but there are plenty of loose-ended goals that are *not* measurable! If you can't answer these questions easily, go back to the drawing board and think about your business's goals again.

CREATING ACHIEVABLE GOALS

This is another one that is probably just as important as creating a measurable goal. Suppose you set goals for yourself that you cannot realistically achieve. In that case, you set yourself up for disappointment, failure, and all-around *bad times*.

I realize this might make me sound like a crazy life coach, but you want to bring positive vibes into your business. If your goals aren't achievable, you won't set that tone.

Ask yourself, *how* can I personally and professionally accomplish this goal? Given my time constraints and general business, is it realistic? When I think about my business's financial constraints, is it realistic within that setting? Is this goal within my ability to complete *right now* or within my *projected* ability to complete it in a reasonable time frame?

Time-related goals are coming in a second, so hold on. But your goals aren't achievable if you can answer no to any of those questions.

I need to pause and tell you it's okay to shoot for the stars. You can dream big in this business, and you can even make it big and live very comfortably.

However, you shouldn't set yourself up for failure right away by making goals that are not achievable *at this very moment*. If you have a Big Grand Goal that you want to be able to achieve, you should instead work to break it up into manageable chunks of goals. Set yourself up with a manageable, realistic *piece* of that Big Dream Goal.

CREATING RELEVANT GOALS

This one is slightly more obvious than the other SMART goals, especially with our business, but I will still touch on it. Creating relevant goals means that your goals are relevant to your business and target market and apply to your personal and business morals.

It's easy to get distracted or caught up in an idea and lose sight of your business or what you want. Is this goal in line with my vision for my company? Is it aligned with my idea of success and where I want to be? Is it *worth* achieving, and is it the right time within my personal or professional development to achieve it?

If you have answered no to these, your goals are not particularly relevant to your business, and you should pause them. If your answers are *not right now, but maybe sometime*, it's okay to shelve them for the moment and come back later when they may be relevant to you.

CREATING TIME-BOUND GOALS

We're at the finish line, I swear. Time-bound goals are important because they give you a deadline, a point in time to work towards. If your goals are open-ended regarding when you can and will achieve them, you may not find yourself having the drive to push for them.

Ask yourself, when will this goal be achieved? When *can* it be achieved, realistically? What can I do, change, or focus on right now to achieve my goal within that time frame? What can I do in the next six weeks or six months?

If you cannot identify *when* you will hit your goals or what you can do *right now* to work towards those goals, it's not a good goal. Go back to the drawing board and rework it.

THAT'S IT FOR GOALS!

I know that felt like a lot. And I'm sure you're sitting here rolling your eyes at me, saying this was unnecessary. But the truth is, it's not! Setting and achieving goals *is* a part of running a business, and you *are* a business owner now. It's just another one of those things you need to get used to doing as a business owner.

Your Target Market

Who are you selling to? Who is going to utilize your services? Who will your clients be, and who will be paying you?

This is something that may evolve and change over time, so feel free to gloss over this point *right now*. You should, however, go back and fill in all the blanks once you are more comfortable in your position and understand your target market. Your target market will drive many things you do, including your marketing and sales.

Product and Service

This one is a little obvious, but this is the section of your business plan where you dive deeper into what you are doing and who you are helping. How does your service work? What is the overview, the main steps, and how are you assisting others?

Positioning

The same freight services can be offered in various ways, situations, and methods.

The combination of these is what is known as "positioning." You must understand what your indirect and direct competition's positioning is.

The more you gather and analyze your competitors and their positioning, the better you can set yourself apart to make your business more valuable. You become indispensable to your shippers, suppliers, and drivers.

Pricing

What is your pricing model going to be? Will you be charging per mile? Per load? Is it going to vary based on who you are transporting for? This is a big question, so just like with your target market, take this seriously and give it some time. Of course, you aren't held in place by your business plan, and if you get deep into your business and realize you need to change your pricing model, that's okay! But go in with a clear idea of what pricing structure you will use and how much you will be charging.

Financial Projections

This isn't easy to write up until you *get* clients and start making money, so this is probably the least important section. Most business plans include this for investors requesting funding for their startup.

What you *need in this section* is how much money it will take to run your business each month, quarter, and year. How much do you have to bring in to stay afloat? What bills and fees will you have to pay?

This is going to be a good guideline for you each month. After a while, you won't have to worry about it because you'll be making far more than you need to stay afloat, but knowing your bottom line is vital at first.

Even if you struggle through this section at first, you should fill it out. If you require a line of credit, you'll need this section – and there is a good chance you will need a line of credit. Most of us don't have the capital upfront to fund the first few months of a freight broker business.

EXIT STRATEGY

An exit strategy is *not* a promise that your business will fail. It's not saying you will, at some point, give up. Instead, it is laying out your options for the future.

If you retire, who is going to pick the business back up? Are you going to sell it? Pass it to a family member? Will you liquidate it over time, or liquidate everything all simultaneously?

These are just things to think about and something to consider. It's better to have a strategy *now* where there is no stress and laying your plan out than having it take you by surprise later on.

Chapter 4: Your Business Details

Once you have your basic business plan outlined, it's time to dig deeper into what it will take to get your business started. This section has information about choosing the right name (it's important!), legally registering your name, setting up your taxes, handling the IRS, and even how to set yourself up with the United States Department of Transportation.

What's in a Name?

Your brand-new freight broker business's name is fairly important, but you don't have to put *that* much thought into it. Before you get your heart set on it and start printing business cards, there are a few things to consider.

The most important thing for your name to be is easy to say and easy to remember. Okay, that's technically two things, but it is still true. Suppose someone struggles to say or even remember your business name. In that case, you probably don't get a lot of word-of-mouth recommendations coming your way. In our business, that's a big deal because many smaller companies *do* talk to one another and communicate.

Most of us use our last or family names, which is valid! It immediately identifies you as the owner and the most important person. It gives you a sense of owner*ship* over the company and brand from the start. It makes a good impression on shippers and carriers alike when they're talking to Thomas Winklefield of Winklefield Brokers or whatever name you have settled on.

Ideally, you will come up with a few top choices for names. That is because yours may be already taken. Bummer, I know.

Once you have a few ideas, move over to your state's business records to find out if it is. These are online in every state and are generally fairly easy to search. Use your desired name and search through the records to see if someone *else* has also thought that was a great potential business name and registered it with the state. If your name is taken, you will want to return to the drawing board and try again.

If your state is cleared, it's time to... yes, continue searching. Go to the county and state trademark records, and search for your name there. If your name is already trademarked, you can't use it for your business. Someone else has, legally speaking, called dibs.

You should also check for similar names, if only for peace of mind. If you're registering "Smith Freight," someone called "Smiths Freight" may be mighty upset with you.

Once you have everything *there* cleared, you can actually move on and register your business name. You need to file a *Doing Business As* or a DBA. A DBA states your intention to do business under that specific name.

To file a DBA, check with your local county website and fill out the appropriate forms. Every state and county will be a little different, but it's usually fairly easy to find and fill out. You'll want to do this in the county you'll be working out of, so most likely whatever your home address is.

What to Register Your Business Under

Once you have your name and business plan down completely, it's time to move forward and start thinking about legally registering your business. There are a few ways to handle this, but the most common ways are doing a sole proprietorship or an LLC. Obviously, there are going to be pros and cons to each option.

Many new business owners gravitate to a sole proprietorship because, on the surface, it sounds like something you would want. When you register as one, you are telling the government that you own this business, take responsibility for it, and do it all – a one-person show, as it were. If you've gotten this far in the book, you probably agree.

Doesn't it make sense to register as a sole proprietorship?

Actually, *no*. While all of that is technically true, there are some major downsides to this type of business. For one, you are on the line if something happens. If the business gets into trouble and goes under for any reason, you are personally responsible for any debts. Creditors can go after your assets, like a home, a car, and more.

In addition, your income and taxes are directly tied to the company. For very small ventures, this can be a good thing and save you time coming to the end of the financial year. Still, a business our size gets very complicated *very* quickly.

A sole proprietorship is not a great choice for our growth and potential earnings.

Instead, I encourage you to register as an LLC or a Limited Liability Company. An LLC is a little more complicated to set up at the start and will initially cost you a bit more money, but it gives you excellent protection.

Setting Up Your LLC

I feel that I've stressed the importance enough, so we're not going to dive into how to set up a sole proprietorship. Instead, I'll walk you through an overview of how to set up your LLC and get your business legal, square, and ready to go.

First, you will want to visit your Secretary of State's website *or* their in-person office. In the last few years, I have found that the less I have to go into an actual office, the better, and more processes are available online.

What you're looking for is the LLC Articles of Organization. This essentially states your intent to start a business, and every state has one. Once it is filled out (and the information varies from state to state but is generally very basic and easy to do), double-check that your state doesn't have any additional requirements.

Once filled out and ready, send your completed Articles of Organization to the Secretary of State's office, along with a fee in their approved form of payment. Again, this fee varies based on your state but can range from $100 to $900. You cannot get around a fee, so budget it appropriately when calculating startup costs.

A Note on Tax Requirements

A handful of states will ask you to pay a corporate tax immediately upon registering. This is fairly rare, though; you usually won't have to pay until you get up and running. Know your state's regulations, though, so you can pay what you owe *when* it's owed.

Speaking of taxes...

Registering With the IRS

Once you're a real, live LLC, it's time to register with the IRS and get your EIN or Employer Identification Number. This identifies you in the eyes of the state as a unique employer, and it is how the IRS will track your taxes. Even if you're *not* going to hire any employees, you must have an EIN number.

Don't feel intimidated by this step! There is a lot of unreasonable fear around the IRS and its processes, but this is actually incredibly simple to do, and the IRS makes it very straightforward.

The first step is to go to the IRS website and locate your specific state's portal. Fill out everything that page asks of you, but *don't* close it. Leave it up.

You will be directed to the IRS main page, asking for more information about you and your business. Fill all *that* out and submit it; it will give you an EIN. Write that down. It's important! You can close this page after you get that number.

Move back to our original page at your state portal, and fill out the EIN information it asks of you. Submit it, and... we're almost done, not quite.

Your specific state should have a taxing authority webpage as well. This is separate from the IRS and federal taxes. Take your EIN and all your documents, and register with your state.

At this point, you may be asked to pay a certain amount of taxes or fees upfront. It varies from each state but usually isn't a lot upfront. Again, this isn't an expense we can skip, so calculate it into your starting costs.

Note: In most states, you do not need a tax seller's permit because you are not selling a good. You're simply a middleman. However, most states are fairly fuzzy on how they legally define a broker and what they consider valid, taxable income. To be safe for your state, you should ask freight brokers you know who work within your state and county or reach out to your state's Department of Revenue and ask. These folks are very helpful, and you shouldn't have trouble finding the answer. Again, *most states* don't require this, but you must be careful.

Getting Your USDOT Number

After you're all legal, registered, and a *real business*, it's time to dig into the specifics of setting yourself up as a freight broker. We start with a USDOT, or United States Department of Transportation, number.

You can do this through the Federal Motor Carrier Safety Administration or the FMCSA main website. This is fairly straightforward and is required by the majority of states. It's important to note that even if you're not working in one of the states required, you may end up working with a shipper that needs something moved *through* those states.

To be on the safe side, register a number.

What is a Broker Authority, and Do I Need One?

Yes, you need one – now, let's talk about what it is.

The FMCSA requires all freight brokers to register with them in addition to just getting the USDOT number. The good news is this is easy to do and fairly straightforward. The FMCSA isn't trying to make your life harder or make this process complicated because people would try to skip out on it if it was very hard.

You will need Form OP-1 or Application for Motor Property Carrier and Broker Authority. This can be found directly on FMCSA's website. You print it, fill it out, and mail it back with all the important information, like your location, legal business name, and insurance information. You will also need your USDOT number.

At the end of this form, you will have a choice. You can register as a "Broker of Household Goods," a "Broker of Property," or both. When writing, it was $300 to register for just one or $600 for both. It's up to you what you choose. Still, I recommend registering for both, especially if you're not sure who your target market is yet. Having the flexibility to take contracts as they come is nice overall.

Some questionable companies will offer to do this process for you *for a fee*. On average, it's at least an extra $75, so they can get the honor of filling out the same paperwork. I don't recommend it.

After your application is finished, you'll get your Motor Carrier number. You're not *quite* done, but you're almost there.

Once you're used an MC number, it gets posted on the Register page of the FMCSA. There is a ten-day span after being posted where someone can protest your registration. This is rare, but it can happen.

Once your ten days are up, you are officially granted your MC authority!

Designate a Process Agent

You need to designate a Process Agent in each state you plan to do business. This includes the state you live and work in and any state where you may pick up a shipper, a carrier, or even transfer cargo through.

A process agent is a person the state courts can legally serve papers to if something goes wrong. Each state that requires one (all 50, plus Washington DC) will need an agent, but you *don't* have to fill out 50 forms.

Instead, freight brokers must fill out one BOC-3 form on the FMCSA website. Only a single form can be on file for any business, and you must also have a copy in your office.

Obviously, this person will be you, the sole employee and business owner. You must complete and file your BOC-3 before moving forward with your company. This form can, like everything else, be found on the FMCSA's website.

Unified Carrier Registration

I swear you're almost done.

The last big step you need to do is apply for a Unified Carrier Registration. There is an annual fee, but it's only $60 annually at the time of writing, so it's not bad. This is the last step; you need your USDOT number to register.

It can be done online at the UCR government website. It's very simple, and the site walks you through it.

How Long Will This Take, Realistically?

This is a big question I get, and the answer isn't a clear one. The truth is it really varies. Each state will have a different processing time based on how many other new businesses they are dealing with, and your own drive and ambition will come into play, too. It can be as little as a few weeks from picking a name to finding clients, or it could be several months if you drag your feet and can't or won't obtain all the necessary information.

It doesn't *have* to take very long and is also not an all-consuming process, so you can keep your day job while setting everything up.

This Seems Overwhelming...

Starting and registering your legal business *can* seem overwhelming, and I completely understand. It's a lot to sort through, and if this is your first business, you might not know where to begin, even with this guide.

Contacting a small business attorney may be a good idea if you feel overwhelmed and can't push through. They can handle the filing and processing of your LLC and all your USDOT and FMCSA information and get you to the end product without much stress on your part. The only issue is that you end up paying not a small amount.

You can absolutely do all of this yourself. I did, and many others do every day. But if you can't emotionally or mentally push past this step, then, by all means, reach out and get help for it.

Chapter 5: Business Banking: The Basics

Getting a business banking account is vital to starting your business. Working from your personal bank account isn't just annoying and difficult. It also makes tax time incredibly precise. With the money we are handling as freight brokers and the insurance we need, a business bank account isn't even a point of negotiation: you *need* one.

Starting a business bank account might seem intimidating for those who have never started a business. It's not! Banks want your business and money and will do much to get it.

How to Set Up a Bank Account

This seems minor, but you must separate your personal and business banking accounts. There are a few reasons why this is true.

For one, the IRS does want to do any extra work. If you *make* the IRS do extra work, they will be very displeased with you. You don't ever want to make the IRS mad at you because that will make your life much harder in the long run.

Sifting through a personal checking account to *find business expenses is almost impossible. At that point, you're not* running a business. It would help if you treated your business like any other business, not as a side hustle. That means opening a real bank account at a real bank.

You *can* open an account at the bank you do all your personal banking in. That doesn't really matter at all. Look for a bank with good rates, deals, extra perks for business accounts, and great hours that work with your schedule. I would love to bank with my local credit union, for example. Still, their hours are so bad I would never be able to *get* there to do anything.

Also, consider ease of use, something many business owners overlook. Do they have an app, so you can easily check your bank accounts on the go? Does the website function well, and is it easy to use? These little quality-of-life things make a big difference when using your bank account daily.

Business Savings: Do You Need It?

When you set up a bank account, you'll be asked if you want to set up a savings and a checking account. With some banks, it comes automatically – you don't have an actual choice.

You might be wondering why you, as a business, need a savings account. That's honestly a decent question, and I understand the confusion.

Most businesses use their checking account for standard daily operating expenses. Your phone bill, internet bill, insurance, and other additional expenses will come out of this account. On the other hand, the savings account is for *storing* extra funds.

This keeps everything a little bit safer, though it does make it harder to access. That isn't necessarily a bad thing, though.

Essentially: the checking account is for bills and everyday expenses. Everything else goes into the savings account.

I always recommend a business savings account, honestly. It usually doesn't cost anything extra to set up, and you have an extra account for storing money when needed. It's fairly standard.

What's a Business Line of Credit?

When you go to a bank to open an account, you may be asked if you want a business line of credit. After having an account for a while, your business may receive letters *offering* you a line of credit. Or, you can go in and ask about it yourself.

A line of credit is essentially a credit card, loan, or another form of credit from the bank. It works pretty much like any other line of credit in your life. There are good and bad aspects to opening a business line of credit or a business credit card.

A business line of credit can be dangerous for those irresponsible with money in their personal life (not judging, just stating facts). It's very easy to overspend using a card; you don't have to think about it much, so my first advice is to know yourself: if you can't handle a business line of credit, don't. However, you'll need much more personal money to run your business.

Utilizing a line of credit is very helpful in our business, especially as you start out. Many times, you are going to need to pay upfront for your carrier. They aren't going to want to wait for your shipper. You may have to cover your trucker's expenses or fees, while your client doesn't have to pay until they *get* the cargo. This can mean you're floating expenses, sometimes many expenses, for the entire time that cargo travels.

When you start out, a line of credit will help you financially float those costs without draining your bank account. It can be scary to see a very low number in your business bank account when you're just starting out, and knowing that you can't cover a surprise expense because of a job you have going on isn't a great feeling.

That said, how *much* credit you get is up to you. There are many factors in determining the line of credit you can get from your bank, including your business's credit information, *your* credit information as a business owner, and the viability of your business. Suppose you are running a questionable or shady business with no direction. In that case, no bank will offer you thousands of dollars just in case.

I highly recommend taking your business plan and all your business information into your bank and talking with whoever they have on staff that specializes in business accounts. If you're going through a smaller bank, you may have to make an appointment, but most of the time, you can walk into a major bank without a huge wait.

Discuss your needs and figure out how much they will be able to offer you based on all of your information. You can also ask how long you have to be in good standing with the bank before they raise your line of credit and how they determine that.

Ideally, you'll hold up to $250,000 in a line of credit. Realistically, most people in our position need at least $25,000 to comfortably pick up unforeseen expenses and handle any costs that come our way. As long as you can be responsible and careful with your line of credit (again, no judgment, just facts), and there are no outrageous fees, get as much of a credit line as possible. This will let you take on bigger jobs, juggle more at once, and ultimately make more money.

It's a risk vs. reward situation, but it's worth the risk.

Do I Need Good Personal Credit?

Here's the thing: yeah, you do, and I understand it's not feasible for many people. If you're determined to start your own freight broker business, you should start working on your credit right now and now. Seriously, start thinking about how you can improve your credit score.

When a bank offers a traditional business a line of credit, they know the business has certain assets they can take if something happens. Usually, it's what the business spent the money on in the first place.

However, freight brokers don't really *have* assets. This is a good thing in many ways because you don't have to stress about managing them. However, getting a business line of credit can be difficult without these standard business assets.

So: yes, you need *at least* decent credit or even be willing to put up personal assets for the business while it is off the ground. Many use their house, cars, or other big assets. This is also risky, so proceed cautiously and be smart about it.

The best thing you can do is work on your credit right now, so you don't have to worry about it later.

CHAPTER 6: BOOKKEEPING BASICS

This isn't a fun chapter for most people. If you have never owned a business, you might not realize how much backend work it is. However, invoicing, proper bookkeeping techniques, dealing with payables... it's actually a lot.

It's not all necessarily hard, so if you feel like bookkeeping is overwhelming, take a deep breath and open your mind before continuing. The hardest part is getting started. As long as you get everything set up properly the first time and know how it all works, it's basically just doing the same thing repeatedly.

Keeping good books and knowing where your money is coming from, and going to, is very important. Some people think you can 'wing it and figure it out as you go, but I promise that is setting you up for total disaster.

Using a Bookkeeping Software

You don't technically *need* to use bookkeeping software. Everything that software does can be manually handled, stored, and filed away. There is a reason. However, most small businesses opt to use the software.

According to statistics released by QuickBooks at the beginning of 2020, 29 *million* small businesses use their software, with about 80% of the market share in total. So... clearly, all of these people think it's worth it.

I always recommend bookkeeping software like QuickBooks, which I use for freight brokers. We have to deal with enough paperwork and juggling, but using software that keeps track of everything, generates templates for you, and makes your life a little bit easier overall is more than worth the hassle of learning it and the relatively small cost to keep up with it.

I will address this entire section as if you are using accounting software. This could be QuickBooks, which is clearly dominating the market, or Wave, which is free but has fewer features, Xero, FreshBooks, Zoho... there are many to choose from.

I started with QuickBooks, so I am familiar with that. I know people who love FreshBooks for their amazing app, so you can manage parts of your business on the go with a tablet or phone. Wave is free but does have payment processing fees.

Do some research if you have *no* experience to see what platforms you like the look of if you're not convinced QuickBooks is worth the money – the very basic program runs $25/month at the time of writing, with the "essentials" plan being $50/month. You can search on YouTube for videos of people using the software you're considering trying out, which should give you a good overview of how it runs and if it's easy to learn.

Another Option: An Accountant

If you *don't* want to manage your own money or accounts or are overwhelmed, you can hire an accountant to help you manage all of this. Depending on your scale, this person may be part-time, working only a few hours a week or full-time, and managing everything. As you start out, you'll only need one on-call part-time.

You can reasonably find a quality accounting to work remotely if you would like or call local accounting firms to see their hours and rates. If you go local, you probably won't be able to find an accountant very familiar with freight brokers. Still, you don't necessarily need someone that is. As long as they understand bookkeeping and accounting, you're fine.

This expense is often too much for new businesses to swallow, which I completely understand. Doing your own bookkeeping is much more work. Still, it saves you a lot of money. It may be financially worthwhile if you are willing to put in the time, especially at first.

Invoicing Clients

You're providing a service that you get paid for. With that, you will need to provide your clients invoices – this is how you get paid. You can't simply call a business and say, "Give me money, please!". You can, but it won't work out for you well.

Providing easy-to-read, easy-to-*play* invoices is essential. If your clients struggle to *give you money*, you have a problem.

The good news is that your accounting program should be able to easily generate invoices and send them directly to your clients. There are also programs specifically for freight brokers that can do the same for you. The bad news is that you'll have to set this all up.

Things you *need* to include on the invoice are the exact rates you charged (per mile? Flat rate? By weight?), the weight of the cargo, a description of the cargo that was transported, the volume or measurement of the freight moved, the *route* of movement the freight took, and any transfer points the freight went through. It should also include the names of the sender *and* the receiver for easy reference.

Good invoicing means sending within a reasonable amount of time and giving your clients a reasonable timeframe to pay before you get upset - usually within a week, but sometimes two, depending on the client and the cargo.

A good accounting service will make this very easy to input and send, so make sure you take the time to learn how to set up and send invoices properly. It will save you a lot of time, and there will never be any confusion about what your billing means -spell it all out.

What Your Bookkeeping Software is Keeping Track Of, Really

There will be features on any software you won't use, but there are some things you need to keep track of. QuickBooks, and others like it, will allow you to easily input a lot of this information and even show you charts, graphs, and print reports with all of this.

You should have all of your assets logged into your accounting software. This includes accounts receivable (AKA, what is owed to you) and the money in your bank account. If you're doing invoicing and payments through your accounting software, this is very easy to do and keep track of. Many services will also tie directly into your bank account.

It would help if you also had all your liabilities within your accounting software. This includes accounts payable (AKA, what you'll owe to folks) and any expenses you have had. Reoccurring expenses, like a phone bill, also count as any office overhead you might have and insurance costs.

All of your income statements, including any payments already made to you, must be recorded.

Essentially? *Any* money, coming or going, should be properly recorded and labeled. That way, you can easily find everything, it is all organized, and you never miss a payment – something you *really* want to avoid.

Save Everything, All the Time

This chapter naturally blends into our next section about taxes. It's hard to talk about one without the other, in fact.

When considering taxes and accounting information, you should save everything accounting-related for at least 3 years. This is not an optional thing you can do; you *have* to.

The IRS can, at any point, decide you did something wrong with your taxes, your accounting, or both and choose to audit you. Auditing is standard, and while it's scary, as long as you follow good accounting, bookkeeping, and tax procedures, it should present no major issues.

I keep everything for 5 years, which is overkill, but it makes me feel better. In addition to everything stored on my computer, any copies of account and tax information are placed in a plastic storage tub, labeled, and tossed in my basement. I have never *needed* that information in those tubs before, but they are there just in case the IRS has questions.

Things You Have To Record

There are a few things that you absolutely have to record. These records are not optional. They are required by law from the Code of Federal Regulations. There is numerous way to record them based on the systems you are using, but you must have on file for every transaction:

-The name of the shipper
-The name, address, and registration number of the carrier
-The bill of lading *or* the freight bill number
-The amount you were paid for your service, and the name of the person who paid you
-A description of any other service you may have performed for this transaction (rare, but it happens), as well as how much you received for this service and the name of the person paying
-The amount of money the carrier charged *you* to ship this cargo and the date of payment the carrier received it

I have a master list of shippers and carriers I always work with, making recording these things easier overall. You can set up your records however you see fit, though. Just be sure you always have these things on file.

Don't Make These (Major) Accounting Mistakes

As I mentioned, taking on your accounting at first can be overwhelming. There are a few *huge* mistakes I see new business owners make repeatedly, so let me go over some of them briefly. You're ahead of the game if you can avoid making these mistakes in your first few months or even years of ownership.

Don't delegate to someone that doesn't know what you're doing. You don't know what *you're* doing? Okay, hire someone or sit down and spend some serious time with your software, learning how to use it. You *never* want to give the accounting responsibility to someone like a nephew, niece, or friend who also has no idea what they are doing.

Ultimately, it's *your* name, *business, and* money on the line. Don't just toss the responsibility onto someone else who has no idea what they are doing and hope for the best.

Could you not put it off? Seriously, don't. So many new owners push off doing their accounting and bookkeeping because it's a hassle, annoying, and boring... and I understand. It *is* boring, I'm not going to lie to you. However, the longer you put it off, the worse it will get, and the less accurate your statements will be.

Always immediately enter information, send invoices, and record payments or transactions. It's just basic, good business practice.

Always properly fill out your invoices. I mention what a good invoice includes above, and you never want to deviate. Honestly, *too much* information on an invoice is better than *not enough*. Your clients should never guess or wonder what they are paying for. Having everything accurate and laid out will help in the long run if you ever have to look up information about a transaction.

Never ignore your liabilities. As mentioned above, this is what you owe. Essentially – any debt the company owes is considered a liability. Beyond being a good, standard business practice, ignoring your liabilities can get you into serious trouble. "I forgot" is *not* an excuse that flies, and the buck stops with you.

Once paid, always clear these liabilities within your software. Don't let paid liabilities linger in your accounts because it *is* easy to forget once the next statement comes, and you're potentially paying twice for something. You don't want to be known as a company that can't keep track of anything.

I Want To Do It Myself... But I'm Nervous

This is a really common feeling. You *think* you could probably do everything yourself and follow a set guideline. Still, you aren't entirely sure and don't want to miss something. There is a middle ground between pushing through it independently and hiring someone full-time.

When you're starting out, you're generally starting small. The best course of action is to hire someone to *set up* your accounting software and walk you through everything you need to record specifically, how to find it, and how to properly maintain your records. This one-time fee usually isn't small, as you're asking for a good amount of work from an accountant. Still, it can give you peace of mind without a reoccurring expense you might not be interested in paying.

Once again, you can contact local accountants or find a freelancer online if you want to go this route.

Chapter 7: Always Be Aware of Taxes

No surprise, but Uncle Sam does not mess around with money they believe is theirs. I cannot stress the importance of maintaining good tax records and keeping everything above board.

Tax audits aren't something everyone can avoid all the time, but by properly filing your taxes and handling your finances, you can make it less likely you will be selected for an audit. More likely, you'll pass if you are.

Even *without* the looming threat of audits, and the IRS combing through every piece of paper, even tangentially related to your business, taxes are serious and time-consuming. According to statistics released by the IRS, the average taxpayer spends about 13 hours *yearly* on taxes, with some organizations and businesses dedicating over 50 hours to the process.

Why am I telling you this? It's not to make you feel overwhelmed or dread the process but to stress the importance of keeping track throughout the year and staying organized. If everything is where it should be, and you know going in what you're doing, tax season becomes a lot less overwhelming.

THE DEDUCTIONS THAT MATTER

Perhaps the greatest thing as a business owner, and handler of taxes, is the deductions. You're paying for a lot of stuff anyway. You might take advantage of as many tax deductions as possible to save money. These small things add up at the end of the year, so I encourage you to take as many deductions as possible.

If you're not familiar, deductions essentially lower your total tax bill. As long as an expense meets the IRS-defined criteria for a deduction, you can claim it as a deduction and pay less at the end of the year.

STARTUP COSTS

If this is your first year in business (and I suspect if you are reading this, it will apply), the IRS will allow you to deduct up to $5,000 in startup expenses for businesses that cost *less* than $50,000 to start. Unless you're doing something very wrong, being a freight broker will not cost you that $50,000, which will apply to you.

Startup costs can include the price of software to get you off the ground, outfitting your home office with what you need, any legal expenses you may have incurred during the time you set up, and even potential office supplies to get running.

As long as you keep records of these expenses, you can turn them in to the IRS at the end of your first year.

Ongoing Business Expenses

Do you have a phone line for work? What about your internet connection? You use that for your business, don't you? Did you purchase a new laptop for work, a second monitor, or a chair? Did you have to take a client to dinner for a business meeting? Do you have business *insurance*?

All of these things are potentially tax deductible. You should keep all receipts and records stored safely, so you can easily access everything when needed.

Taxes on Commission

This probably sounds like a dumb statement, but you *will* have to pay taxes on the commission and income you bring in. Some new owners don't understand this, so it bears saying!

You need to report your commissions annually so that the IRS can accurately track how much you owe. You should always set aside a portion of what you are making in your business for quarterly tax time because you never want to be hit by a surprise bill from the IRS.

WAIT... QUARTERLY?

Surprise! You are a business owner, and tax time isn't just annual for you; it's *quarterly*.

Suppose you are classified as an independent contractor or a self-employed worker. In that case, you must file quarterly taxes on your income with the IRS. Because there is no automatic tax withholding system, you essentially are tasked to do it yourself.

The IRS asks you to take your business expenses, deduct them from what you have made, and pay taxes on that amount. You also may have to pay self-employment tax. You are estimating what you will make and pay taxes on that.

You still have to file annually, and if you have overpaid, the IRS will issue you a refund, just as if you were a W-2 employee. If you have underpaid for some reason, the IRS will ask you to pay the difference.

Suppose you are not an independent contractor but a W-2 employee of your business. In that case, you shouldn't have to pay quarterly taxes.

What If I Forget?

It happens; life gets busy, you don't realize the date, and suddenly you have failed to pay your taxes by a scheduled deadline. This is *not* great, but it has happened to many people. Don't think you can wait until the next deadline to pay the appropriate amount.

The IRS will not forget that you forgot this payment. Contact them immediately to set up a rectified payment schedule. Fees are often involved, depending on how late you are and how much you owe, as what extra fees you will deal with.

You only have to handle those fees once before making it a priority to file.

Big Mistakes New Business Owners Always Make

There are a handful of easy-to-spot mistakes I see people making with their accounting that leads to fees, audits, and a lot of headaches.

Estimating or Rounding

If you're doing a lot of driving, you might end up rounding your miles up or estimating. Suppose you're spending a lot of business dinners or other expenses. In that case, it's usually "easier" to go with a close estimation.

However, big round numbers set off all sorts of flags with the IRS. I know keeping track of every mile and drop of gas is a pain, but getting yourself audited is much worse. Nothing will set off an audit like a "10,000 miles driven" flat.

Miscellaneous Deductions

There is a section when calculating deductions that are considered *miscellaneous*. This is where anything that doesn't fit into a specific section or area goes. You should be careful using this section and treat it almost like a trap.

If you regularly put large transactions within the miscellaneous deductions, you ask to get audited. Always do your best to file everything where it belongs, and treat this deductions section as a last resort.

Beware Home Office Deductions

Remember how I told you that you can classify many of your home office expenses as business expenses so they become tax deductible? That is completely true, *but* be aware of what you are deducting.

Many new business owners read that they can write off part of their mortgage payments and utility bills as a business expense and go crazy, but this will send many red flags. Suppose you want to deep dive into all your home expenses that qualify as business expenses. In that case, you need to keep detailed records.

Calculate the square footage of your office, and use that as a guideline. If your home office area is 10% of the home, you can deduct 10% of your home heating bill as a business expense. This applies to all household utility bills, like water or gas, and your property taxes, HOA fees, and trash removal.

This *does not* apply to expenses that have no direct impact on your business, though. You can't deduct what you are paying your lawn guy to come twice a month and do the grass because that isn't interacting with your business. Renovating your kitchen brings no value to your business, so you can't include that.

Should I Do My Taxes Myself?

I've included many places where you can cut corners and save money by doing something yourself or simply going without until you can afford it. That is because I think there is enough room in this market for everyone, and there's no reason to try and box someone out because they don't have or don't want to spend a large amount of money upfront.

That said, I *highly* encourage you to spend the extra money to get an accountant to come tax time.

The IRS is complicated, and there are many loopholes you may have to jump through for everything to go right and correctly pay your taxes.

It's not complicated because the IRS is being a jerk. By its nature, it is simply a lot to deal with.

An accountant used to handling small businesses and their tax needs will be your absolute best bet for getting the correct information to the IRS and avoiding an audit.

CHAPTER 8: INSURANCE 101

Insurance: a business owner's best friend and that is a fact.

Insurance isn't just something that you are required by law to have. It is something that can seriously protect you. If something goes wrong, decent insurance will cover you completely, and stand up for you in court, worst case situation.

Many new business owners try to squirm their way out of insurance or pay for the cheapest insurance they can find because it's an "extra expense." In my experience, it's not an "extra expense." It's a *vital* expense, and getting a good insurance plan covering you completely is very important.

Do I Really Need Insurance, Legally Speaking?

Not only is it good to cover yourself, but it's also the *law*. **All** freight brokers working in the US are legally required to have a $75,000 surety bond or trust fund. Generally, this is done through an insurance company. This surety bond exists to protect you and your clients. If you, as a freight broker, don't live up to your promises or contracts, this bond tells your clients that you *have* the money to cover losses.

When you get your surety bond through your insurance company, they will file the proper paperwork with the FMCSA. You only have to obtain the bond. You generally don't have to do much else with it – though you should let all of your prospective clients know you *are* bonded.

Choosing an Insurance Company

Put that phone down. Don't you call your local Geico agency! You might be able to get business insurance through your current personal insurer, but they might not have the best rates for you. Instead, I recommend you look for a local or national insurance company that handles businesses like ours.

An insurance company that is used to handling accounts like this will know how to properly file with FMCSA, will know how to handle any issues that may arise, and will have agents who can walk you through issues or processes without any hassle. When you're considering agents, ask them if they have any freight brokers with them and if they understand the surety bond (sounds like a dumb question until your agent says he doesn't know what that means... yes, that has happened to me!), and how they handle an issue with cargo resulting in their involvement.

Choosing an insurance company is important, but it's also good to know that you can change anytime. Read your contract closely before signing, and know when you need to renew it versus when you can leave it. If you're unhappy with your current insurer, you are not stuck! Never let your insurance, or your surety bond, lapse, though. That is a surefire way to see trouble.

General Liability Insurance

General liability insurance is fairly standard for all businesses. I highly recommend it for *every* new business, not just freight brokers.

Generally, liability insurance covers your business's *equipment* and any property you have from... well, most things. Fire, theft, natural disaster, anything like that. It also covers any damage done by an employee of yours... which would be you in most cases. However, if you spill a big cup of coffee all over your laptop keyboard, insurance may be able to reimburse you for a new one.

If a fire happens in your home and some of your equipment is damaged or destroyed, your business insurance may cover that.

This is also the insurance policy that covers you against *lawsuits*. There are a thousand reasons why someone may 'come after you legally, and none of them are fun to deal with. If this happens and issues arise, you call your insurance company, and they handle it, from talking to their angry party and their lawyer to actually representing you in court if it comes to that.

This is a huge weight off of many owners shoulders, and it can't be overstated how important it is. It only takes one single time, one issue, to wipe a bank account clean, not to mention how stressful the process can be personalized.

In short? I can't recommend general liability insurance enough; everyone should have a good policy.

Business Interruption Insurance

This is the first discussion on the insurance that isn't technically necessary but is important. Business interruption insurance is really nice to have, and it's great for peace of mind.

This type of insurance covers partial or full business expenses if something happens that causes your business to shut down. This could be property damage, like your house catching on fire and destroying your office, long-term illness, or even death. Liability covers the *damaged goods*, while interruption covers the *business expenses* when you are out of work.

We all hope that we will never need such an insurance policy coverage. Still, if you do, it's incredibly nice to have. Not having to stress and worry about paying all of your monthly expenses in full when something goes terribly wrong can mean the difference between your business continuing and your business shutting down.

How Much Should I Pay For Business Insurance?

This is a question that I can't necessarily answer specifically. The cost of your business insurance will depend on several factors, including where you live and where you run your business.

In my experience, comprehensive business insurance with your bond can cost anywhere from $2,000 to $5,000 yearly, generally paid quarterly to your insurance company. So, for your first quarter in business as a startup expense, you can expect to pay $500 to $1,250 to your insurance company.

This seems like a lot, but insurance is legally required, so it's not an expense you can get around. It is also great, and I never complain about paying my insurance company. A quality insurer will have your back.

Shop Around Regularly.

Honesty, this is just good standard insurance advice, but you can and should regularly shop around for different insurance providers. Based on how long you have been in business and your past claims, you may be able to save a ton of money by switching to a new insurance company. The same applies to your car and homeowners insurance as a little life pro tip.

Just follow all the good practices for *choosing* an insurance company, and you're golden!

Side Note on Insurance Policies

Just as a note on insurance policies, I highly recommend you read *all* the fine print on a policy before you sign on the dotted line. Some of this risk is mitigated when you go with an insurance company that is comfortable with freight brokers and has insured them.

However, you should always read the fine print on your contracts, ask questions about things you don't know, and thoroughly understand what to do if something goes wrong. What is it the insurance company will do to cover you? What are your rights? Do *they* have the right to void any claims? How do they pay out, and how long do they have in their contract to do so?

Understanding this top to bottom is *so* important. You don't want to discover in the middle of a problem that you don't have the coverage you thought you did!

Chapter 9: Your Home Office, the Most Important Place

Home is where the heart is.

Well, in my case, home is where the work is. For you, too! A home office is essential to your future success, and having a good area to work and focus on will make a big difference.

Can you run this business from your bed with a laptop and coffee? I mean, technically, sure. I've even had "off" days where I've been sick enough to feel bad but not sick enough to not work, and I've done paperwork or made calls from my bed, propped up with pillows.

But long term, you will want a professional, clean, organized office space. There are a few reasons for that.

This may not apply to everyone, but it is important to note it just in case it applies to you. I struggled to work from home until I had a dedicated space to work. It's hard to shift into "work mode" when you're sitting at home on the couch, with the TV in front of you, the Xbox controller to your right, and your phone on the table, wearing pajamas and snacking on cereal.

It is much easier to get into "work mode" when you're sitting at a desk you use for work, with all of your papers and tools near you and most of your distractions in another room, away from where you can see them.

Within my own morning routine, I get up, flip the coffee maker on, and change. I wear comfortable clothes, but I personally can't work in pajamas... I can't take myself seriously with my Batman fleece pants and hoodie. Jeans or slacks and a t-shirt or polo are more than enough for me.

I do my bathroom routine, get my coffee, make breakfast, and eat with my wife. Once I'm ready for my second cup, I take that to the office and close the door.

Closing the door in my house means it's work time. Clients don't want to hear my dogs barking, my wife's meetings, or my kids crying. It's unprofessional at best.

Once I am in my own office, I'm ready to work. This is my place of work, and mentally I have switched to *work mode*.

Where to Put Your Home Office

You might not have a big enough home right now to have a dedicated room for your home office. With housing prices the way they are, I honestly understand. However, you do need a dedicated *space*.

If you *have* a spare room or a guest bedroom, that is a great place to put your home office. A corner of a finished basement no one uses also works great. However, I highly recommend making sure to bring a sweater... I get cold after a while sitting at the desk.

I have even seen successful freight brokers use their garages or sheds on their property. Bring a fan for the summer and a space heater for the winter, and you have a separate area where you can work without being disturbed.

If you *don't* have a dedicated space to close the door and only do work in that area, you should start looking for the next best thing. Can you turn a corner of your dining room into an office with a desk? What about part of your bedroom? Worst case situation, but the living room might even work, depending on who else you are living with. If you have kids, I recommend choosing a room with a door.

No offense, but no one wants to hear Coco Melon while talking to you on the phone.

YOUR "WORK STATION"

Your workstation will be the most important thing in your office. It's where you will sit daily, make phone calls, and handle your business.

You don't need the most expensive desk in the world, but get something big enough to fit at least one monitor, keyboard, mouse, and paper. I do a lot of "jotting down" notes on the phone longhand because it's easier to write with one hand than type, so having a little extra space makes a big difference. There are a few options for a decent desk if you're on a budget.

The first option is second-hand. Check out your local thrift stores, scour Craigslist and Facebook Marketplace, and look for a decent, sturdy desk big enough to suit your needs. Depending on the area that you live in, you may be able to find a desk far better than what you could reasonably afford new.

Another thing to consider is somewhere like Ikea. Their desks are good, but you can also buy a tabletop the size you need and 4 legs to go with it. My very first work desk with this, and it came to less than $50. After using it for several years, I finally replaced it after I got tired of not having drawers.

A chair is next, and I recommend buying a new one. Find a chair that is rated to sit for a long time and is comfortable for your own body. I need one with a headrest for comfort reasons, but other people may have different needs. Sit, test, and try chairs. You can get away with a cheap one for a while. Still, in my opinion, a decent computer chair *is* a necessary expense.

You spend a lot of time sitting in this job, be it doing paperwork, making calls, or working on your marketing... your body should be your number one priority. A good, supportive chair will mean less back pain in the long run.

Your computer will be your lifeline, so you must have something reliable. A laptop is fine, but make sure it's not falling apart or is very old. It should have enough RAM to easily run the software you'll use (more about that soon) and be relatively new. Ideally, it will not chug through a simple Google search or preparing documents.

I personally use two monitors. This gives me plenty of screen space to move documents and chat windows around. I can always have my email up in a window and never feel like I have lost a tab, page, or document. You don't need two, especially at first, but it is nice.

A SIDE NOTE ON ERGONOMICS

As mentioned just a few paragraphs ago, we spend much time at our desks. I encourage you to adopt healthy, good desk habits now, especially if you're not used to this work. Sit up straight, shoulders back, with both feet on the floor. Keep your wrists slightly elevated from the keyboard and your arms straight. Set your monitor, so it's a comfortable eye height.

You never want to wreck your body from a job, especially not a desk job. This might not feel natural if you're used to doing more manual labor or traveling for work. Try to get used to it, and you'll save yourself a ton of discomfort, pain, and medical bills.

Just ask my chiropractor.

Extras You Absolutely Need

Your biggest work friend, besides your computer, will be your phone. Your phone will be a lifeline, allowing you to make contacts and schedule everything. Do you have something to consider when using a landline or cell phone?

Now, it's not 1982, so you're probably shocked I even suggested a landline. However, they're very common in this industry, and many guys I know still have their old landlines kicking around.

The only time a landline is a better choice than a cell phone is when you have terrible cell reception in your home. Some people live in the boonies and can't get a clear call to save their lives. In this situation, maybe a landline is a good idea.

A cell phone gives you a lot more flexibility. A big benefit of this job is you can really do it from anywhere, so if you get to the point where you want to pack up your laptop and work stuff and head to the beach for a week or six months, your cell phone can easily come with you, and you won't suffer any disruptions. While you may be able to set up call forwarding on your landline, it will be a lot more complicated.

Suppose you have poor cell service but good internet. In that case, you can also consider a provider like Google Fi that will allow you to make calls using your internet connection, giving you better call quality while you are on WIFI.

Speaking of the internet, another absolutely essential part of your home office is *good* internet. You don't need the best business-class internet to let you download 30 gigs of data in 5 minutes, but you shouldn't cheap out, either. Fast, reliable internet is *essential* to our position, and it's important that you can easily access the internet barring natural disasters.

THINGS YOU MAY NEED

These are all I have and utilize, if not every day, at least most days. You may not need all of these, and you may not need them immediately, but they are something to consider.

I have an essential combination of fax, scanner, and printer, and I use them constantly. Again, it's not the 1980s, but many businesses you will be dealing with are smaller, older, and potentially antiquated. They may be different to deal with than a newer, sleeker company, but their money spends the same. Having a working fax machine means I can get and send documents quickly and easily to these companies.

I also have a filing cabinet to file forms, documents, and contracts for future reference. It's a little old school for me, but not *everything* is digital all the time, and I like staying organized.

In addition to that, I have a shredder to dispose of unwanted, potentially sensitive documents. It saves stuff from piling up, and I know it won't be found and potentially used by someone else. I know most of us to have the attitude of, 'who would even go through our trash,' but it *does* happen!

Tips for the Best Office Space Possible

As I mentioned, creating an office space where you can focus and work is *very* important. You might think I am exaggerating if you have never worked from home. Still, the environment really does make a difference for most people.

My office is painted in neutral, calming colors, mostly blues and greys. Nothing bright or distracting. I don't have a television in my office, though I do regularly listen to music while I work. There's a difference in my working brain between having a TV show and music – some guys can happily work with sports or talk radio in the background, though. You must figure out what works for you and not allow distractions to get the best of you. After all, *you* are in charge of how much you can accomplish and therefore make.

CLEAN WORKSPACE = CLEAN MIND

Staying clutter-free is also very, very important. The messier your desk and office are, the harder it will be to find what you need when you need it. This can lead to many issues when answering shipper or carrier questions or figuring out what you need for the week.

A cluttered space also *feels* overwhelming. You might not notice it at first if you are generally a messy person (no judgment, I am absolutely known to pick up clutter in my personal life!), but working with a clean space is like working on a blank slate.

At the end of every day, I clean my desk of anything I don't need. Papers get shredded that I don't need, everything gets filed away I'm not going to use first thing in the morning, and I leave my desk in a neat, clean state, ready for the work day tomorrow. Any mugs for coffee, glasses for water, or plates from lunch get removed. This takes less than ten minutes, from deciding I'm done with work to leaving my office. It also saves me hassle in the mornings, and I know I won't have to stress.

Over time, you will develop your own routine to combat clutter and keep everything organized. Still, it would help if you did so sooner rather than later. It only takes one big mistake with a client, losing documentation, or making yourself sound stupid on the phone before you realize staying organized is the way to go.

SEPARATION MATTERS

This is an important thing to consider if you have an active family. I've touched on it earlier, but you need a way to let people in your household know you are *at work* and can't really be disturbed. There's no way the person on the other side of the doorway knows if you're on a call and dealing with an issue or just futzing around.

No matter how well you outfit your office or how much time you put into getting the perfect desk, you're not worth a lot if you get interrupted on the phone every day.

Make sure you have that vital separation in your home. It's *so* important to remain professional!

A Note on Hours

You are your own boss here. You make the rules and procedures, including your office hours. You can set your own office hours and technically work when you want.

Remember that standard *business* office hours are 9-5. I find many companies I work with run an 8-4 or even 730-4 schedule, so I start my mornings a little earlier than some. I recommend choosing hours that fit your lifestyle – never set up when you're so tired you can't open your eyes and choose hours you can come in.

Once you set your hours, you should work hard to stick with them. Make yourself reliable. If people know you're supposed to be at the office working by 9 am, don't leave all your emails unread and your phone unanswered until noon without a good reason. I keep saying these words, but it's unprofessional, and you *will* lose money from it.

Do you need to be sitting *at your desk* for your full work hours? That's a little bit fuzzier. Probably not, honestly. I always keep my work phone on me during work hours, with the volume up. My email is connected to my phone, so I can respond to calls or check my emails anywhere. On slower days or in the afternoons, I often run errands, grab the mail, and do a load of laundry... all normal things.

So, you don't *have* to be at your desk, though you should be *available*.

Turning Off

If you choose to work beyond or outside of your work hours is up to you. I am not your parent or partner, so I cannot tell you what to do. However, I recommend setting boundaries. You don't need to be connected to your phone and your business every night.

Once you set your hours, stick to them, and learn to step away when they are through. Shut your office door, put your work phone on the charger, and only check it perhaps once or twice throughout the night if you feel the need. This is a lot harder as you're starting out, and you feel like you're clawing your way to success, but the longer you go on, the more important it will become.

A good work-life balance will keep you in this business for longer and make you happier, both very important things.

Chapter 10: Software That (Might) Help

I preach about being open to technology and embracing it in many parts of this book. We have finally hit the chapter where all of that comes into play.

Software is going to be a huge part of your daily routine and life, and finding software that is easy to use *for you* will make a big difference in how much you get done each day, how efficient you are when you're working, and how happy you are at the end of each work day. There's no worse feeling than fighting with the program you're trying to use.

However, choosing the program or programs to use can be overwhelming. I won't lie to you here (well, I'll never lie to you, especially not here). There are a lot of programs on the market to choose from. Many developers over the years have realized that logistic-based operations like ours really do need the help of great software and have put on various choices for us to use over the year.

Why Software, Anyway?

A lot of folks that are new to this business seem to think using software is unnecessary. You *technically* have to use very little software to do your job, but that's such an old-school way of thinking.

The truth is software makes our jobs easier and more enjoyable. Good software will take a process that would normally take an hour and take ten to fifteen minutes. You can track shipments, keep up with your shippers, and find new shippers and cargo, all within a quality software set.

Think about it this way: as a freight broker, you juggle many things. Invoices, carriers, shipments moving, finding shippers... it can be a lot. It's only natural that if you try to do it yourself with no outside help (in this case, outside help be software), you'll let some things fall through the cracks. With good software, things are *far* less likely to fall through.

This is where my tip of being flexible, adapting to new things, and learning comes into play. You will never make the money you should be made without it; that is just a fact.

What Are Some Features a Good Freight Broker Software Has?

There are a few things to keep in mind when looking at the different programs on the market. This will apply to any program you look at at any time – so if you're reading this several years after I write it, this is all still what you should keep an eye out for.

Load management is an absolute must for good software. You should be able to track your loads, the drop dates and times, the carrier, and what is on each and every truck, boat, or plane. In addition, it should store that data for quite a while – this makes figuring out what carrier you used for a similar cargo later on a whole lot easier.

Document management is an absolute *must* in my experience. There is nothing better than having all your documents properly digitized and stored right in one place, with a system that lets you search, compare, export, and print without hassle. Make sure whatever software you use has a quality management system – and bonus points for letting you easily transfer digital documents from one computer to another, like a shipper or carrier to you. This will save you so much time.

If your software has **route planning or dispatching**, you pick a good one. The software has come a long way. Many will now help you plan the most efficient route using common traffic data and leave times and even help you plan where your trucks will stop for gas, given the price. This can help you figure out the best *carrier* for the job and keep your carrier payments to a minimum.

Many good freight broker programs will have **invoices** built-in, so you can easily send your shippers an invoice and handle customs or payment issues. This isn't strictly *necessary*, but it's becoming more and more common, and I really do love it. Some will even fully replace a system like QuickBooks and keep track of your accounting issues, payment schedules, expenses, and so much more. Just be careful when utilizing it, as missing something during your accounting processes can mean a big headache regarding taxes.

What Software to Choose?

This is tough, and the answer can change depending on whether you're reading this chapter ten days after I wrote it (impressive) or three years later. I will give you an overview of some of the most popular software on the market *at the time of writing* and some features they have.

To write this, I am not only pulling from my own experience with this software, but I called around to see what other people used and read reviews online. Hopefully, this will help give you the best 'picture' of the software.

ASCEND TMS

A quick Google will tell you that this is one of the most popular software for people in our business. It's a relatively 'generic' supply chain management software. It includes some nice features, like integrated maps and GPS tracking for some carriers.

Ascend is nifty because you can get access from anywhere and set different payment methods for carriers - by mile, by load, etc. Ascend also utilizes TruckStop for load searching and can help you find carriers with its database. It's easy to use, and in my experience (and in reviews I have read), their customer service is great.

At the time of writing, Ascend TMS is free for the "basic" package, which is more than enough to get your foot in the door and play around with it to see if you like how it is set up. You get just two users with the free package, but that's generally not an issue in our line of work.

The premium version is $79 per person per month - again, in our line of work, *especially* at first, you're only going to need one person: you! In addition to everything that comes with the basic package, premium users get 15 extra features, like the ability to export your load reports, a *ton* of accounting options (enough that you probably won't need a program like QuickBooks), and really great document management services.

Before you buy, check the database of carriers in your area for the type of shippers you want to service. In my experience, the database can be hit or miss, and it feels like it is not always as updated as others on the market. This may be an issue with what I am moving or where I am, so dive into the free version thoroughly.

DAT BROKER TMS

This software boasts that it was made "exclusively" for freight brokers. Maybe 10 years ago, that would have been a good flex, but now much of the software on the market was made first and foremost for freight brokers like you.

Like others on our list, DAT has a pretty solid layout of features for users. They have their own load board, a user-friendly data management system, and an accounting section of the software for accounts receivable and analytics (so you always know what you're making and where your money goes). You can also easily track your cargo and see when it's been loaded, where it's going, and when it gets delivered.

DAT has mixed reviews online, which I found interesting because, in my experience, I only had a few issues. For one, depending on the time of day you're trying to work, their load boards are a little... unreliable. Not great in our line of work, and you may find yourself refreshing. Getting the "perfect" search filters set up can also be cumbersome, but that may be more of a preference situation.

At the time of writing, DAT Broker TMS costs $100 a month for their entry-level package, which is more than enough for most users. Other, larger packages are available, but you won't need that many users unless you're running a large freight broker company. There is no free trial and no free version.

ALJEX & DESCARTES

This one is very popular with mid-size freight brokers and gets great reviews due to the daily tasks you can automate. Making some of the more 'mundane' actions of the job automatic can free up your day and give you a lot more time to focus on the things that are actively making you money.

Like many on our list, Aljex & Descartes has accounting software built-in. You can send invoices and track orders; it has advanced route planning and a great reporting system. You can also easily create a profile for shippers or carriers, quickly reference anything else you have done with them and give them the best ongoing service – a big plus when building a reputation and connections is so important.

At the time of writing, Aljex & Descartes costs $290/month for the base program. You can 'upgrade' to additional tiers at $550/month and $1050/month. Still, most of these features are for larger companies that manage many employees, so it wouldn't give you a ton of benefits to pay extra. There is no free trial and no free version.

Being the most expensive option on the list, you may wonder why I'm even bothering to include it. Aljex & Descartes indeed comes with quite a hefty price tag. For many of you starting out, it's an expense you can't justify. I *absolutely* understand that. It's important to include it, though, because it really is a premier option. It's user-friendly, has a lot of great tools, and is widely used. I mean, *Pepsi* uses it to handle a lot of its logistics operations.

If you want the best of the best, many freight brokers will tell you this is it.

ROSE ROCKET

To close out this software section, I will include software I've had my eye on for a while. Rose Rocket is one of the newer programs on the market. It has many of the best features that Aljex & Descartes does, like automation of the 'boring' stuff. It also can automatically generate quotes, track shipments across the US, and give you complex reports on where your money is going.

A big benefit of Rose Rocket is the mobile app. It's incredibly user-friendly, runs just as well as the full version, and lets you monitor shipments on the go. If you have to run to get coffee, do errands, or get out of the office, the app will help track what is happening.

Rose Rocket also boasts that they integrate *many different platforms into their software, giving you access to more carriers, shippers, and* services. This is true, but in my experience, it's also the biggest downside to the software. When I write this, the integration isn't flawless and sometimes feels sluggish. The developer team does seem dedicated to making a polished final product, though, so if you stick with it, you will be rewarded.

At the time of writing, Rose Rocket costs $80/per month per user. There *is* a free trial and a limited free version, so you can test it before you dedicate yourself completely to this software. I recommend at least making an account and seeing how the features work.

How Do I Choose?!

Read all that, and are you still confused?

I recommend setting aside a bit of time and going to YouTube. Type in each freight broker software you're thinking of trying and look for a hands-on video of someone *actually using* it. I can talk to you about the software until my voice is gone. Still, there's almost nothing better than seeing someone else use it.

It truly comes down to your personal preference. What do you like the look of? What seems easiest for you to use? Suppose you want to use software because it's the best-reviewed or what the professionals use. In that case, that's fine... but if you find it clunky or difficult to maneuver, you will avoid using it. Ultimately, you won't see any benefits at all.

Go with what feels *right*, and you'll get much more out of it.

A Note on Organization

Multiple times so far, I have told you how important it is to stay organized. One way you can do that is by utilizing technology.

I highly recommend using a calendar program that easily syncs with your phone, tablet, or whatever device you use most for your business. Accessing your calendar on the go and from anywhere, including your home office, is practically essential.

I use the integrated Outlook calendar, which works on any platform I need it to, including just a browser. Every date I need recorded for whatever reason is stored there, including invoicing notes, outgoing payments, and so much more. It's essentially the hub for my business. There are also freight broker programs on the market which have a great app that can sync to your phone and let you see everything you have going on at a glance.

A huge benefit I never thought about until I needed it is that you can always access what was done previously. I can go back to dates and see what I had scheduled, what was happening, and what I was *doing* in general. This type of record can make a big difference if you ever encounter an issue.

You don't have to use Outlook, but a system is important. I also have a physical calendar in my office, hanging on a wall for important dates and reminders. However, digital backup is supreme.

CHAPTER 11: GOVERNMENT REGULATION AND FEDERAL LICENSING

Below is a list of the basic compliance requirements you need to obtain and maintain to operate your freight broker business.

FEDERAL COMPLIANCE REQUIREMENTS FOR FREIGHT BROKERS

The "Code of Federal Regulations (CFR), Part - 371 - Brokers of Property" is the law regulating the freight industry. There are several requirements that freight brokers need to adhere to, as well as a set of special rules and regulations for those who ship household goods and products. Below are the steps you must take to be licensed.

STEP 1: REGISTER WITH THE STATE AND IRS

The process for you to become licensed starts with registering your business in the state where you are going to operate. Since this is a home-based business model, you will want to register in the state in which you reside.

Each state has its own set of procedures for registering your business. Check your Secretary of State's website for the specific rules and filing fees.

Once you have filed your business registration with the state, you will want to get an Employer Identification Number from the IRS to have a proper business tax registration.

Registering your business will involve determining the type of structure your business will have.

Corporation, Partnership, Sole Proprietorship, and LLC (Limited Liability Company) are your business structure options.

STEP 2: REGISTER YOUR FREIGHT BROKER LICENSE WITH THE UNIFIED REGISTRATION SYSTEM

Before December 12, 2015, new freight brokers were required to also register with the FMCSA, the Federal Motor Carrier Safety Administration.

The FMCSA offers free training to help you step by step through the application process.

STEP 3: COMPLETE THE OPERATING AUTHORITY APPLICATION

One of the first things you will need to do when applying for your license is to apply for operating authority. This is also known as the MC number.

This number and your "operating authority" are just what they sound like. This is your authority to operate this freight brokerage firm from home.

You can choose from 2 different operating authorities as a freight broker. Which type you choose is going to be dependent upon the types of cargo that you will be transporting and arranging.

You do not have to choose one over the other. If you choose to operate as both authorities, you allow yourself room for more income.

Each application must have the fee paid, which will be discussed in Chapter III.

The two types of operating authority are:

-Property Freight Brokers

-Household Good Freight Brokers

Suppose you also want to offer carrier services in your freight brokerage firm. You must visit the

United States Department of Transportation and obtain a USDOT number.

STEP 4: GET YOUR MC/FF NUMBER AND GRANT AWARD

After you have submitted your application, you will get an MC/FF number. FF numbers are assigned to freight broker designations, and the MC number is for all other carriers and brokers. The type of authority you have applied for will determine if you get just one or both of these numbers.

This is one of the most vital pieces of information about your business. You will want to keep this number secure and easily accessible.

Remember that this number is not your operating authority, and your application is not considered complete until you have received your official grant award by certified mail.

This award is the certification/documentation of your MC/FF number. While the grant letter is being sent to you, your operating authority application will be published in the FMCSA Register.

This publication starts a 10-day countdown period where you have to wait for your application for operating authority to be challenged. This challenge can be by any person or company who thinks that you should not be given this authority and want to stop it.

STEP 5: GETTING YOUR FREIGHT BROKER SURETY BOND/TRUST AGREEMENT

The BMC-84 bond is the bond required to start a freight brokerage firm. It offers financial protection for you and the clients that you serve. It basically is a guarantee that if you do not follow all laws and regulations or cause any damage or loss to a company, they have a legal right to file a claim against your bond to recover their losses.

The BMC-84 Bond is $75,000 in value, which is now a minimum requirement as of October 1, 2013. The bond must be obtained from a licensed and reputable surety bond agency. These agencies will work on your behalf with the bond issuers and backers.

The amount with which you can obtain your bond is going to be dependent upon your credit score, your finances, and other financial factors.

You will receive a quote based on those factors. For those with good credit, that quote typically ranges anywhere from 1-5% of the total bond amount

Once you have found a company to issue you a bond, as required by law, they will automatically file all necessary documents with the FMCSA on your behalf. You will get copies of the filing for your records.

STEP 6: OBTAINING FREIGHT BROKER INSURANCE

It is a federal law that all freight brokers hold freight broker insurance if they also plan on operating as freight carriers and forwarders. You do not have to obtain insurance if you only operate as a broker.

You will want to get cargo insurance as a broker. This way, if there is damage to a shipment, it's not taken out of your bond. It is also recommended that you get general liability and property insurance coverage.

Suppose you will hire employees in your business and pay taxes on them. In that case, you will need workers' compensation insurance for each employee. You will need to be verified with your State.

Your carriers are going to need to have workers' compensation insurance themselves, even if you do, too. If they are exempt, they can provide you with a written statement for your records so you are covered.

FMCSA Regulation 49 CFR Part 366 is the law that requires all freight brokers to list each process agent that they are going to use in each state where they have an office or plan to write contracts and do business.

Record Keeping and Accurate Accounting Requirements

The FMCSA and the Department of Transportation are the regulatory bodies that oversee this industry. They require that each freight broker keep accurate records of every single transaction, which is each shipment/load, for up to three years.

Each record must contain the name, address, and phone number of the sellers, shippers, and carriers. You will also need to keep each BOL (Bill of Lading) and how much you were paid for your services for each load.

Bond Renewal Laws

To remain compliant and in business, you must mark your calendar with two extremely important renewal dates. These are your FMCSA information and your freight broker bond.

FMCSA Registration and Authority Renewal/Update

Whenever you have a change in any of the following, you must notify the FMCSA:

-Your business designation or registration

-The status of your operating authority, adding a new authority, or removing an authority

-Insurance policy limits and terms

-Equipment and location changes

Aside from changes, you must keep in touch with the authoritative agencies every 2 years. Thirty days before you are due for an update, they will send a friendly reminder via postal mail.

FREIGHT BROKER BOND RENEWAL

Freight broker bonds will need to be renewed each year on the anniversary of its effective date of surety.

If you do not renew your freight broker bond, you will violate the laws and compliance regulations set forth by the FMCSA. That could result in your license being revoked or suspended.

It can also be revoked for repeat instances of renewing and failure to maintain it consistently.

Chapter 12: Getting Your Online Presence (Plus Online Marketing 101)

We live in the future, folks, and no one is anyone without a website. My mother started a website a few years ago. While I understand getting off the ground initially may be intimidating, it's *not that hard*.

We also have to talk about social media and why it matters. Are you a 14-year-old girl? I'm assuming not. This would be a strange personal interest of yours. You may think this social media is only for kids and teenagers, but it's important for all businesses. Let's get started.

Creating a Site

The website will be the foundation of your online presence, so getting this part right is important. You want your website to speak to your client and share why they should choose you to handle their cargo.

For many shippers, the website will be your *first impression* with a client. You won't really be meeting these people face to face. You're going to be talking online and over the phone. The website should be their first look into what you have to offer.

Your website must be professional, easy to find, navigate, and use. It doesn't have to have a ton on it, and it doesn't have to be complicated. It just needs to *work*.

"Websites are *so* expensive!"

Not necessarily! You're *not* going to be doing anything like selling products, and you don't need a lot. You can buy a domain name for about $20 upfront, with an annual renewal to keep that name as your own for about $15/year. Hosting is anywhere from $5-$25/month.

WEBSITE PRO TIP

Never use a "free" domain site like Wix or Weebly. It *seems* like a great idea, but it looks incredibly unprofessional. Your URL will be yourbusinessname.weebly.com, which looks like you don't know how to manage a basic website. If you can't manage a website, how are you supposed to manage cargo?! I would never trust my cargo to someone with that URL!

That said, Weebly apparently has a 'professional' grade design side that will let you use your URL, and I have seen some folks get great results. I personally have never used it, so I can't comment one way or the other.

IT DOESN'T HAVE TO BE HARD

Many people get caught up with the idea that creating a website is hard or complicated or you need to know advanced coding. You don't need any part of this, I promise you. Technology has come a long way since then.

You're going to first have to choose a hosting site. NameCheap is my personal favorite, but friends of mine swear by Blue Host – there are many out there. I would personally avoid Go Daddy, as I've had bad experiences with them, but use what you like and what you can afford.

The domain name needs to be purchased upfront as well. Most hosting sites will help you with this! If possible, you should go for your name or something like your business name, freight broker. Simple, easy to remember, easy to type, and a reflection of you and your actions is a perfect choice.

Once you have your domain name and hosting taken care of, it's time to put WordPress on your site. Again, every hosting company will handle this differently, but with NameCheap, it's only a few extra clicks.

WordPress has become much easier to use since it first debuted, and that's great news for you, who is developing a site. There are literally thousands of templates to choose from. If you don't like the handful, the initial WordPress setup has offered you, simply Google "free WordPress themes," "cheap WordPress themes," or "WordPress themes for a business." You're going to get an overwhelming number of options.

Choose a theme that you like the look of, that suits your business, and is inoffensive and easy to navigate. You can install free or paid themes through WordPress on your site.

Alright, now it's just time to modify what you have there! You can add custom logos, headings, and page titles and change up the basic information like the *About Us* section. I'm going to touch on this in a moment.

The one thing I think is an old-fashioned, but still worthwhile, thing to do is to write a blog. Make it a priority to write at least a weekly post, and write about what you see in the industry. It could be shipping across state lines, contacting carriers, your favorite software, or even your absolute best work efficiency tip.

This is going to help drive traffic to your site. It will show potential shippers you know what you're talking about and add more bulk to your site.

When writing your About Us section, don't lie, but you won't admit it if you don't have overwhelming experience. Expand on your knowledge, what you have, and what you have to offer your potential shippers.

A NOTE ON YOUR WEBSITE

You would think this is another thing that doesn't need to be said, but you would be surprised. Always create *original* content. You should never completely lift something from a competitor. Your blog posts, marketing materials, and every aspect of your website should be unique.

Never take something someone else created and pass it off as your own. You will look like you don't know what you're doing and fraud or scammer at worst. *Not* a good look.

What Does SEO Mean, and Do I Need It?

SEO stands for Search Engine Optimization, which is how search engines like Google or DuckDuckGo find your website. It's all based on keywords.

Think about if you were to search for, say, "best restaurants in Miami." The results will be articles that use relevant terms to the discussion. The same goes for if you are searching terms like "best freight broker in Kansas" or "freight broker in Oxford."

The truth is, though, SEO is complicated, and it's not always easy to pull off naturally. You might be able to jam a blog with keywords, but picking those keywords can be tricky, and making them sound natural is even harder.

Suppose you want to generate organic leads through your website. In that case, you should consider either taking a short course on best SEO practices or hiring a professional to help optimize your website. This can be a one-time hire or a reoccurring package with someone.

"Why can't you teach me?!"

Could I teach you the best SEO practices? Yeah, and it would be about the length of this book. It is also an ever-changing market, like how Google and other engines handle keywords and indexing. It's much more complicated than you might think and would take far too much of your time.

If you are interested in it, I encourage you to dive deep into that world. Website Learners and Ahrefs have excellent YouTube videos of varying lengths that will give you a crash course *and* offer longer, in-depth discussions on the topic.

Should I Hire Out My Website Creation?

Like many other things in this book, if creating a website is a sticking point, you should hire someone to set it up for you and transfer ownership. This can range from a few hundred dollars to a few thousand, depending on how complex you want your website to be.

You can use a company dedicated to website creation or find a freelancer willing to help on a website like Upworks or Guru. You *can* do this yourself, and it's not all that hard, but if you do not have the time or the confidence to do it, you should outsource it. Outsourcing and getting it done is far better than avoiding it or doing it without real intention or effort, giving you a poor final product.

When you hire someone, make sure that they understand your vision and have the same goals for the website as you do. That is, you need to have your vision clear and be able to explain it *to* them. Find a variety of sites you like the look of, and give them plenty of vision and direction to go on.

The Logos, Branding, and Graphics That Matter

A good, professional business has a professional logo in several sizes for different applications, a professional letterhead, and professional graphics. You are a professional business, and you need these things.

There are a few ways you can accomplish this.

The most labor-intensive way is to do it yourself. Websites like Canva exist to help you design a decent graphic, or you can hit up YouTube for some basic Photoshop tutorials that may help you get where you need to be.

You can also ... hire someone. Much like website creation, there are a variety of options for professional graphics. I like using something like Fivver, personally. Good graphic design isn't *that* expensive when you consider the amount of time and skill that goes into it. For not a whole lot of money, you can get a lot of options and support a freelance graphic designer somewhere.

If you hire someone, just like with a website, it's important to have a clear goal in mind. Go to the designer with ideal colors, designs, and logos that you find appealing - several, ideally. Are you looking for sage green colors and your initials? Let them know! Rose gold with a truck? Sounds great, but make it clear to the designer.

By doing this, you are saving their time by not having to do revisions and saving them time and money.

This is one of those personal things where I know my strengths and weaknesses, and I know I don't have the patience or the visual design skills to make my own. However, if *you* have that, make your own! Save that money!

Do I Really Need Social Media?

I understand that you may be hesitant to have a social media platform. The truth is, you don't have to do a *ton* with it once you have started. Share articles or news in the business, share any blog posts you make and communicate with potential shippers.

You're going to want a Facebook business profile for sure. This also means you need a personal Facebook page, at least, to manage this - if you don't have one of those, start it now.

To create a business page from your PC, open the Pages icon on your main splash page and hit Create New Page. Name your page the name of your business, add a category, and fill out all the important information, like business hours, contact information and more.

You can later add pictures, like your impressive graphics, and more information about your business. It will be a little bare at first, but the more you use it, the better it will be. Make sure to add a link from your web page to your social media.

Twitter is another one I would encourage you to have. It's just as easy to make a new account. You can and should follow the accounts of shippers you regularly work with, carriers you like, other freight brokers, and companies you potentially *want* to work with in the future. This is a great little networking tool that more people in our business should utilize.

Is Coke going to pay attention if you follow them? *Of course not*. But a smaller local business that needs to use a freight broker certainly will because you know their social media person is wearing half a dozen hats.

Just like with your Facebook page, you should post fairly regularly. You can also interact with like accounts and build relationships through social media that may translate offline. It doesn't have to be a lot – a like here, a comment there, just little things now and again.

I'm going to say you *aren't* getting a lot out of something like Instagram, which is mainly a picture-based way to communicate. Still, if you want, you can also create an Instagram account. It works like Twitter; you can share information and photos and interact with other companies and brands.

I have never utilized TikTok, and I don't see the benefit in sharing videos of my day. I'm either working on something boring or handling sensitive information for the average person. I'm *not* going to blow up my shipper or carrier on social media with what I'm doing for them that day, so I don't know if I would get many benefits.

That said, you absolutely *can* make a TikTok. I recently read a news article about someone who is a Microsoft Office expert. All they do is share videos about using Excel and Microsoft Word in better ways. They bring in six figures a year between their videos and the consulting jobs they have gotten *from* those videos.

If you make and use TikTok, be smart about it. We handle a lot of sensitive information, so never share your shippers, carriers, or their specific cargo with any identifying information. To make the best videos, use a good-quality camera, either an actual camera or a recent high-end phone. Avoid offensive or unprofessional language; be kind in the comments sections.

Remember that your TikTok is not just a reflection of you as a person but your business. If a shipper considers using your service and Googles you, they *will* find your social media pages. Suppose your TikTok is full of things that do not reflect on you well as a professional business owner. In that case, there is a good chance that the shipper will take their money and cargo elsewhere.

In short: Fun, silly dances are fine, but be professional.

Chapter 13: Finding the Carriers, and Shippers, to Succeed

You'll need to find shippers and carriers to build lasting relationships. You mustn't consider just how to strengthen those bonds but how to find and build them in the first place.

Good marketing matters, and knowing how to market yourself and attract potential clients also *matters*. This will be the overview of finding, securing, and keeping good contracts with shippers and carriers. Hence, you always have a supply of fresh shipments waiting for you and a line of eager and interested carriers that want to work *with* you.

Think About Interactions

I tell every single new business owner this: *think about it*. When you call a new business for the first time, how do you expect to be treated? How would you expect to receive that service if you were to walk into a new business looking for a specific service? How would you want someone else to talk to you?

It's so easy to get caught up in the day-to-day business dealings that we forget we're not just running a business but a customer-centric business. You want to give off a professional aura and ensure people know you want to take care of them. I've said it a hundred times in this book, and I'll say it a hundred more before we're done. The customer experience matters and you need to be sure that you treat every customer as you would want, with a professional attitude.

Referrals Are King

Referrals, word of mouth, and recommendations are truly what is going to propel your business to success. Suppose Business A has been around a long time and interacts well with you. In that case, they will talk about it to Business B and Business C, with whom they have a good working and personal relationships. I know this because my father-in-law owned a steel fabricating business for his whole life, and he would talk shop *all the time* to other business owners in the community.

I also know this because I get a *ton* of work simply from doing my job well at an earlier date. It's going to blow your mind the longer you're in this business, the more you realize just how rare that is.

Don't be afraid to ask for referrals, especially starting out. If you have given exceptional service and know everyone involved is happy, it isn't out of line to ask this; it can really help. If you have a good connection with the shipper or a business, it's also okay to name drop – "I've worked with X business for a while now. If you're unsure, feel free to reach out to JimmyBobJones there, and he will happily provide a glowing referral."

Should I Cold Call?

Look, cold-calling sucks. It really, really sucks. When I started my business back in the day, I did a lot of cold calling, introduced myself to local and regional businesses, and made connections. It *sucked*.

Did it work? Well, yes, kind of. I started a conversation leading to jobs and still work with some companies today. However, I'm not sure that the effort I put in was worth the results. I feel that cold calling maybe even less effective today. We truly do business differently.

Instead, I suggest something like a *warm* call. Look for a list of distributors or manufacturers in your area, and take some notes. What do they make? What do they ship? Are they large enough to have their freight broker under them, or are they small enough to need someone like you? What is their revenue?

Once you're armed with this very helpful knowledge, you can start your "warm" calling. It's still technically cold calling because they didn't express interest in your business. Still, you have much more information about the company and its needs. This will help you get your foot in the door and land those contracts.

Should You Send Mailers Out?

Talk about old school. Mailers have been around for a thousand years in the marketing world. They *can* work, though... as long as you're smart.

What you don't want to do is spend an absurd amount of money on direct marketing. If you're spending $1,000 or more on mailers for a handful of companies, you're doing something wrong.

There are only a few key pieces to a good direct mailer.

You should include an introduction letter, saying, "hello, how do you do." Introduce yourself, your business, and what you do. This should be on your letterhead with your logo and include your website, phone number, and email address.

It should also have a small bit of marketing with it. This could be a pricing sheet, references to past clients, your mission statement, all the services you can offer your shipper and how much easier they can have it... think about how you are making their lives better, and capitalize on that.

If you have a decent color printer, you can print these out yourself or take them to a printing company. Even Staples or a FedEx store (I almost aged myself here and said Kinkos!) would be able to get you good-quality prints, especially for what you need. Then, stuff your envelopes, label them, and send them all off!

You can always follow this marketing up with a call to check-in. Introduce yourself, tell them you sent them information, and ask if they require your services or have any questions. There is always a chance your mailer goes straight into the trash, and you get told they do not need you on the phone. That's okay, and that is part of it.

Mailers are a slow game, so send them out with some regularity but *not* annoyingly. Once a month at the most, and be sure to change it up a little bit each time for some variety. You want your name to cement itself in your potential shipper's mind when they think freight broker – this is why you get all those mailers during holidays, simply saying "happy holidays." Reminding customers they exist!

Email Mailers

Anything you can send in the mail can *also* be sent via email. This is the way to go if you're starting out with a tight marketing budget. I wouldn't double send (as in, send the same company a digital and physical mailer). Still, you can cover more ground by doing a combination of both.

You'll want to send everything you sent via mail, including your introduction letter and a piece of marketing to explain who you are, what you have to offer, etc. You have more freedom to add more since you're not paying to print and mail it.

You should have a call to action at the end of any mailer, email or print. This is essentially prompting the potential customer to contact you for their business. The best calls to action should be relatively subtle but clear. This could be a popup when you go to close the window, prompting the customer to reach out, or a link at the bottom to contact you for more information. Experiment with similar sites to see how they handle a call to action.

Note: Some important things to include in any mailer are that you are insured, bonded, etc. This seems obvious after reading this book that you would have to be, but it's not always so obvious looking from the outside. This can help give your potential shippers a bit of peace of mind.

Can I/Should I Use Load Boards?

Load boards are an online marketplace and system where shippers can *post* cargo that needs to be moved from point A to point B. A carrier can see it and go. Oh, I want to do that and pick it up. Some load boards are free to use, others have an upfront cost, and others have a monthly subscription. There are *many* load boards to sift through, and some freight broker software we discussed previously has direct access to load boards built in.

You might think that a load board is essentially a freight broker in digital form, and you wouldn't be wrong. However, many busy shippers and carriers don't like using them because they have to handle their own paperwork and manage everything themselves.

You can use a load board if you choose, and it can be a good way to get your foot in the door, build connections, and set up a good reputation for yourself.

For a good reason, Convoy is probably the most popular load board on the market right now. It's easy to use and navigate through and doesn't make your job harder. You don't have a limited number of searches; you can search through every state and easily see carrier reviews and ratings.

The biggest downside to Convoy is the price. At the time of writing, it was $100/month. It will pay for itself once you get everything set up and start pulling in jobs, but it's certainly a monthly investment until then.

Truckstop is another cheaper option – plans start at $39 at the time of writing and have a fairly large network. It was one of the first major load boards to take off, so it has some history. It's good for newbies who don't want a big financial investment and want to get the feel of a load board.

There *are* more advanced options, but you have to pay for them.

Finally, I'll recommend **Direct Freight**. They have been around for over 20 years and may be the best and cheapest way to get your foot in the door and see how load boards work. The monthly cost is just $35 at the time of writing, and they have a lot of advanced features that are just *nice*, like saved searches, weather reports, and more.

If you really don't want to pay, **PostEverywhere** is one of the better free load boards on the market. Its concept works around last-minute transportation, but that's not all there. In my experience, PostEverywhere is good for beginners who are figuring it out and those who really don't have the budget. Still, it won't be the only load board you ever use. It doesn't have many bells and whistles that the other boards have.

Again, you don't have to use any load board, but you should never *ignore* an opportunity to make connections!

Online Advertisements

When I say *adapt to technology*, I'm not **just** about creating a website and using new software. I'm also talking about marketing your business, and you can do that by making online ads.

It's not that scary, I promise you.

I won't overwhelm you with information, but let us look at the issue on the surface and see how you can start building, running, and using ads to bring in new shippers and make some money.

GOOGLE IS KING

Google Ads have been around almost as long as Google has, and they're popular for a reason; they are easy to use, not wildly expensive, and they work. People trust Google. Depending on your target market and how you want to find shippers, Google Ads can be a great tool.

Google won't target specific people with advertisements. Instead, they target specific *keywords*. Suppose you know your potential shipper is searching for a "freight broker in Oklahoma," for example. In that case, you can target these keywords and show your website to anyone that searches that.

Here are a few key things to remember when setting up a Google Ad. One is the landing page, or where people go if they click on the ad. Make sure your landing page is relevant to the ad that you posted. If people are searching for freight brokers for their specific market, take them to a page that shows you have experience in that market.

When choosing your specific keywords to target, think about what potential shippers might be searching for. Don't be so broad that you're competing with an overwhelming number of results, but don't be so narrow that no one is searching for it.

I recommend thinking of potential keywords and then searching Google itself to find the number of results you get. "Freight broker near me" gets 91 million results at the time of writing, with the top ad being Amazon. "Freight broker in Ohio" gets over 2.8 million results, with *zero* of the top results being Google Ads. That's a good search term to target – people are searching for it, but no one has any ads running. "Freight Broker in Cleveland, Ohio" gets over half a million responses, with zero ads.

You can see where there is a big opportunity for you to jump in here and get some of this internet traffic, right?!

Before you ever complete an ad, do a once-over to ensure you have filled out *all* of the information and everything is up to date, both on the ad itself and your actual webpage. This is something a lot of people miss, but it can make a really big impact on the final ad.

RUNNING SOCIAL MEDIA ADS

This is a little bit riskier in our line of work. Still, you can run advertisements on your social media pages if you feel it would benefit you. Running social media ads is very easy, so don't feel intimidated.

First, you must choose the post you want to advertise with or 'boost' as Facebook calls it. You should choose a well-written, engaging, and interesting post

After you choose the post, you can pick your target demographic (usually age, gender, and general geographic region) and then choose how much money you want to put into the post and how long you want it to run. Once you've done those things, let it go and watch the views happen.

This is the standard process across the board. You can also promote your business *page* through Facebook, where people in the market you choose will see your business page, an image of your choice, and a little blurb about your business. Again, this is a great way to get your name and exposure.

I wouldn't waste too much time or money on social media marketing, as it still tends to be a less surefire method for our business. Still, I have seen some success with thoughtful, smart social media marketing.

If you want to learn much more about social media marketing, the School of YouTube has plenty to offer you. Most of it won't be specific to freight brokers and will probably not apply to our business.

Chapter 14: You Can Fail... or Thrive: Major Issues You Might Run Into

Beyond what I have already included in the relevant sections of this book, there are some major (and minor) things I see a lot of new brokers do that are serious issues. Even some veterans make these mistakes.

Knowing they are mistakes before you jump in and how to prevent them from happening will give you the *best* chance of success. We all make mistakes occasionally, but knowing what a mistake is and how to fix it fast can make a big difference.

Not Vetting Your Carriers

It's so important that you use trusted, reliable carriers to move *other people's* cargo. Always remember it's not your stuff you're moving around the US, it's someone else's, and it should be treated with respect.

The biggest mistake you can make is not vetting your carriers and not regularly rechecking to ensure that the carriers you are using are still up to snuff. Your shippers are also going to ask you about how you vet your carriers, so having a system in place that is unique to you can help. I always check safety ratings, online reviews if possible, all qualifications and certifications, and discuss with the carrier about *what-if* situations and how they handle it, like what if a truck breaks down somewhere.

I always impress upon my shippers that I thoroughly vet my carriers. At this point in my career, I mostly only work with carriers I have been using for a long time. I'm very friendly with dispatchers and employees there, so it's not an issue. As you start out, though, you need to be extra sure.

Even with that friendly attitude, I regularly ensure all carriers are still compliant!

Trash Your Reputation

I've said it a thousand times, but this is the biggest mistake I see people making in our industry, so I want to nail it home for you. You must maintain a good reputation that shows you are professional, easy to work with, and reliable. Shippers look at you as a freight broker, like they are adding you to their staff. You wouldn't hire someone with a bad reputation.

While starting out, you might feel like you are at a disadvantage. It's hard to build up your reputation from nothing, after all. The best way to start is by networking with other brokers or industry professionals.

You can also join trade associations to help build your reputation, like the Intermodal Association of North America or the Transportation Intermediaries Association. This little seal can go on your website, and potential shippers can look your name up in the trades database to find you. This adds another layer of reputation and trust.

Maintain Your Online Footprint

If you go this far and completely skip over the part about setting up a website and social media page... go back and do it.

Would you hire a company to transport something important to you if you couldn't find *anything* about them online? Of course not. That is so sketchy! Having an up-to-date online footprint will give shippers confidence that you can handle their goods and that you are a real person and company, not just a voice on the phone.

Undercut Carriers

It's easy to dream about making the big bucks immediately. Still, I see new folks making a huge mistake when they enter the industry is trying to undercut their carriers to pad their bottom line. This goes well with reputation, but the fastest way to stop having quality carriers is to not pay them what they are worth.

Make sure you research the average load costs and what the market asks. Always offer your carriers a reasonable rate that leaves them money, too. Obviously, the market is always changing, so this is something you need to keep up with – you *will* have to adjust rates as time goes on, but that is just part of the business.

Treating Carriers Poorly

Again, this goes hand in hand with my previous point. Still, it's become somewhat common for freight brokers to treat carriers poorly over the years. I want to make this crystal clear, no matter what else you read on the market: while the carrier is technically working for you, you are not their superior, you are not their 'boss,' and you do not get to order them around, talk to them like they are less than you, or otherwise be a jerk.

This is a great way to ruin your reputation with the best carriers on the market and end up with no one wanting to carry your loads.

I'm going to take this a step further and tell you to research the laws and regulations of your state. Check the Hours of Service regulations, and note the maximum hours a driver can work without a break, how many breaks they should be good for good practice, and how much sleep a driver needs to have. Write this information down and keep it somewhere handy. Always follow these regulations, and ensure your drivers understand that this is what you want from them: good driving practice.

Will your cargo take very, very slightly longer? Sure, maybe – but it will get there on time, in one piece, with a healthy and safe driver. You never want to put your driver's life at risk.

You are responsible for ensuring your driver has enough time to get the cargo where it needs to be. Your responsibility is to protect your driver and anyone else on the road who may be traveling during that time. Never assign impossible or even difficult schedules. If you have a deadline that is only met with an impossible driving schedule, you have made a mistake somewhere, and your inability to plan is *not* your driver's problem.

They aren't your subordinates, nor your slaves. Treat them with respect, and you will be shown that same respect.

Don't Do Illegal Things

Well, that's a big statement. You should always be honest and transparent with everything you do and avoid doing anything illegal.

A few years ago, a guy I knew got busted for doing *double brokering*. The carrier (the gentleman I was familiar with) agreed to transport a load. Instead of transporting it, though, he offloaded it to *another* carrier. **This is illegal,** and the government doesn't appreciate it when it happens. The paperwork was a mess, nothing was done right, and he lost all accreditations. He's no longer in the business, as you can imagine.

Stay above board, never compromise your morals for a quick buck, and only take what you can handle. You never want to be known as an untrustworthy or unreliable freight broker.

Keep Track of Your Financials, Always

In our business, throwing around a lot of money is easy. 30k for a delivery? Sure, I'll put it on credit. $50k to a carrier? Let's go. This is a big payment.

It's also easy to get carried away when you're new to this kind of money. Always stay on top of your balances, know when your money is coming in and from who, and never spread yourself so thin that a single payment or transaction can make or break you. This is how you get into seriously deep situations and take on more to try and make a quick buck... and then something illegal or untrustworthy happens.

It gets easier to keep up with this sort of thing as you go, but when you start out, make it a priority to always know where your money is going, who has it, and when you're getting more.

DON'T LISTEN TO OTHERS

You are going to run into people in this business who cut corners. You'll find impatient shippers who don't understand why their cargo is taking so long to move and want you to make it happen faster. You will find carriers who skirt safety regulations and push their drivers too hard. You'll find other freight brokers giving you the advice you *know* isn't right, but they always do it.

DON'T LISTEN TO THESE PEOPLE.

It might "work for them," and you may see what they are doing and think they are working on easy mode or have it all figured out. They don't, and I promise it will come crashing down around them. It's your job as a business owner to navigate these challenging people diplomatically to run your business above and beyond.

Conclusion

There's no question that the last few years have been hard on most businesses. With a global pandemic that shut down trade routes, decimated many manufacturing facilities, and stopped work for millions, it's a wonder we are now bouncing back.

However, the shipping industry took far less of a hit than many other industries. Everyone still needed goods, and they needed them shipped far more than before since the average person couldn't travel far.

The outlook for our industry is excellent, and projected growth is very promising. As I said at the very start, there is more than enough room in this market for you, me, and anyone else reading this book. We can all have a piece of this pie.

This book was written with my experience, a lot of additional research, and an eye to the future. What the landscape for our business will be in the next ten years, no one really knows, but it looks very good.

Starting a business is a big choice for many people. It takes a lot of guts, a lot of confidence, and a whole lot of drive. If you don't have that drive to get out there, help people, interact with customers, and make money daily, this may not be for you. I'm not trying to be rude or crush your dreams, but *you* have to be able to push yourself to greatness. No one else will.

There are always risks when starting a business, especially when discussing handling as much cash as we do when working as a freight broker. However, with great risks comes great rewards. Following my guides, taking your time, and learning as you go, you will set yourself up for a minimal-risk, maximum-reward situation.

Hopefully, with this, you have learned how to become a freight broker, run a business, and consider yourself a businessperson. Remember, this is not a get-rich-quick scheme, nor a way to print money. So many younger folks try to break into this market and think they can start making six figures within a few months. It may work at a time, but it's not good for your reputation, and your long-term future will hurt.

Be patient, go slow, build connections, and *put in the work*. This is a business where, if you put in the work, you will see the fruits of your labor, no question about it.

I hope this book has helped you understand what it takes to be a good freight broker. Keep your head down, and keep pushing, and I look forward to working with you.

Appendix: Terms That Matter

Accounts Payable
Your accounts payable are the accounts that *send* payments, like paying a carrier for their services.

Accounts Receivable
Your accounts receivable is the accounts that *take* payment, like receiving money for shipping cargo.

Audit (IRS)
If the IRS determines that you have incorrectly filed your taxes or misrepresented the amount of money you have made, you may undergo an audit. This is when the IRS goes over all your paperwork for that fiscal year to determine if something was misrepresented.

Bill of Lading (BOL)
This document is given to the carrier when the cargo

is picked up. This is all the necessary information for the shipment, like the delivery location, commodity, and weight.

Business Interruption Insurance
A type of insurance covering partial or full payments while the business is stopped for reasons beyond your control, like a fire or flood.

Business Plan
A business plan outlines your intention to start a business and where you see the business going.

Cargo
Cargo is anything that is being moved or transported.

Carrier
The carrier is the transportation company moving the cargo from point A to point B.

Cartage
This is another term for cargo.

Claim
A claim is made against the carrier for lost or damaged cargo during transport.

Common Carrier
A common carrier works on an as-needed basis for anyone willing to pay.

Consignee
The opposite of the shipper, the consignee, is the person receiving the cargo.

Consigner
Another term for shipper.

Contract Carrier
A contract carrier usually works on a long-term contract with a single or select few companies.

DBA
This stands for Doing Business As, or your business name will be.

Delivery Receipt
A document signed at the time of delivery, noting the cargo has reached the destination.

EIN
This stands for an Employer Identification Number and is how the IRS designates you as an employer.

Expedited Shipment
Freight that needs to be moved faster than standard delivery, normally for an additional fee.

FMCSA
This stands for the Federal Motor Carrier Safety Administration.

Freight Broker
A middleman that works with shippers and carriers to move goods from one place to another.

General Liability Insurance
A type of insurance that covers overall business items, like computers and phones.

Global Freight Forwarder
Companies that handle shipping across countries.

Gross Weight
The total weight of everything being transported into any pallets or packaging material.

Guaranteed Shipment
For an additional fee, a guaranteed shipment is when cargo is promised by a set time.

Insurance for Freight
This is a system setup where the shipper or the broker agrees to pay an additional premium in case of damaged or lost cargo. This additional layer of security is rare, as carriers hold their own insurance policies for this reason.

Interline
This is the process of using *multiple* carriers to get the cargo where it needs to be.

Intermodal
Using multiple methods to transport cargo, like a ship and a truck.

Line of Credit
A credit line is given to your business from a bank, like a credit card or loan.

LLC
LLC stands for Limited Liability Company.

Load Board
An online system that helps connects shippers, freight brokers, and carriers.

Merchant Navy
Boats owned by a government that transports cargo overseas.

Net Weight
The weight of the cargo without packaging materials or pallets.

Process Agent
A person designated by the company will be served papers by the state if something goes wrong.

Pooling
Pooling involves combining multiple shipments into one truck to save on transportation costs.

Proof of Delivery (POD)
See Delivery Receipt.

Safety Rating
Carriers have safety ratings based on how many miles have been driven without minor or major accidents. It essentially is a way of seeing how well-run the carrier is and how secure the cargo will be.

Shipper
A shipper is someone who has cargo that needs to be moved.

Shipping
Commonly accepted as any form of transportation,

shipping *technically* means to transport cargo by ship specifically.

Shortage

A shortage is when the delivered cargo is less than the picked-up cargo.

Surety Bond

Also called a trust bond, this type of insurance freight brokers must have.

Tariff

In shipping terms, the tariff is any rules or agreements between the parties involved.

Third-Party Billing

Rarely the shipper or the consignee will not pay for the shipping costs. Instead, it is handled by a third, outside force.

Tracing

Tracing is simply tracking a shipment through its standard route.

Transit Time

This is the time the cargo is in transit, from when it hits the truck to when it lands at its final destination.

UCR

This stands for Unified Carrier Registration.

USDOT

This stands for the United States Department of Transportation.

PAGE 19
PAGE 24
PAGE 25

Printed in Great Britain
by Amazon

60748384R00090